MAYER SMITH

When I Met Her

*Copyright © 2024 by Mayer Smith*

*All rights reserved. No part of this publication may be reproduced, stored or transmitted in any form or by any means, electronic, mechanical, photocopying, recording, scanning, or otherwise without written permission from the publisher. It is illegal to copy this book, post it to a website, or distribute it by any other means without permission.*

*This novel is entirely a work of fiction. The names, characters and incidents portrayed in it are the work of the author's imagination. Any resemblance to actual persons, living or dead, events or localities is entirely coincidental.*

*Mayer Smith asserts the moral right to be identified as the author of this work.*

*Mayer Smith has no responsibility for the persistence or accuracy of URLs for external or third-party Internet Websites referred to in this publication and does not guarantee that any content on such Websites is, or will remain, accurate or appropriate.*

*Designations used by companies to distinguish their products are often claimed as trademarks. All brand names and product names used in this book and on its cover are trade names, service marks, trademarks and registered trademarks of their respective owners. The publishers and the book are not associated with any product or vendor mentioned in this book. None of the companies referenced within the book have endorsed the book.*

*First edition*

*This book was professionally typeset on Reedsy.
Find out more at reedsy.com*

# Contents

| | | |
|---|---|---|
| 1 | The First Glance | 1 |
| 2 | Shadows in Her Smile | 4 |
| 3 | Letters Without Names | 8 |
| 4 | A Walk in the Mist | 12 |
| 5 | The Edge of Memory | 18 |
| 6 | The Edge of Truth | 24 |
| 7 | The Shattered Reflection | 30 |
| 8 | The Weight of the Truth | 36 |
| 9 | The Echo of the Unseen | 42 |
| 10 | Into the Shadows | 48 |
| 11 | The Secrets Beneath | 55 |
| 12 | Fractured Memories | 62 |
| 13 | The Unseen Hand | 69 |
| 14 | Beneath the Surface | 75 |
| 15 | Into the Abyss | 81 |
| 16 | The Silent Watcher | 88 |
| 17 | Beneath the Surface | 95 |
| 18 | The Echo of Lies | 101 |
| 19 | The Weight of Shadows | 108 |
| 20 | The Cage of Truth | 115 |
| 21 | The Mirror Shattered | 121 |
| 22 | The Shifting Faces | 127 |
| 23 | The Echo of Her Name | 133 |
| 24 | The Descent into Silence | 139 |

25  The Final Awakening                                   144

# 1

## The First Glance

The air in the café was heavy with the scent of freshly brewed coffee and faint traces of vanilla from the pastries in the display case. It was a place he rarely visited, but the chill of the December wind had driven him inside, seeking warmth and distraction.

Jason settled into a corner seat, his laptop open but ignored, his hands wrapped around a mug of steaming coffee. The hum of conversations around him was soft, almost lulling, until the door chimed. He glanced up.

That was when he saw her.

She walked in like she belonged to another world entirely—a dark coat brushing her knees, her hair loosely tucked beneath a beret. But it wasn't her attire that caught Jason's attention; it was her face. Something about the way her eyes scanned the room made his chest tighten. They were searching, probing, as though she carried a secret she couldn't quite share.

Jason's gaze lingered as she ordered at the counter. Her voice was soft, but there was a firmness to it, as if every word she spoke was deliberate. When she turned to find a seat, their eyes met.

For a fleeting moment, the world around them seemed to pause. It wasn't a look of recognition—he'd never seen her before in his life—but there was something there. A flicker of curiosity, maybe. Or was it unease?

She chose a table not far from his, setting down a small leather-bound notebook and a pen. Jason tried to return his attention to his screen, but it was impossible. The way she held the pen, tapping it lightly against the notebook, seemed oddly familiar.

Then she began to write.

Jason couldn't help but steal glances. Her hand moved swiftly across the page, her brow furrowed in concentration. Occasionally, she'd pause, her eyes darting toward the window as if searching for inspiration—or reassurance.

He wanted to say something. Ask her what she was writing, maybe. But there was an intensity about her that made him hesitate. Instead, he watched, pretending to type as he tried to piece together her story in his mind.

She glanced up suddenly, her eyes locking with his again. This time, there was no mistaking it—she had noticed him watching.

Jason opened his mouth, an apology forming on his lips, but

she smiled faintly. It wasn't warm, exactly. It was the kind of smile that hid more than it revealed.

Before he could speak, she stood. Gathering her notebook and pen, she walked toward the door. Jason's heart raced—was she leaving because of him?

But as she passed his table, she paused. For a moment, he thought she might say something. Instead, she slipped a piece of paper onto his table and walked out, the door chime ringing softly behind her.

Jason stared after her, the paper untouched for a moment. When he finally picked it up, his hands were trembling slightly.

Written in precise, elegant handwriting were two words:

"Don't forget."

Jason read the words over and over, trying to make sense of them. Don't forget what? He didn't even know her.

Yet, as he sat there in the now-empty café, a strange certainty settled over him. Whoever she was, this was only the beginning.

# 2

## Shadows in Her Smile

Jason couldn't stop thinking about the note. It was tucked into his jacket pocket now, but its weight felt far heavier than the paper it was written on. Don't forget. The words circled his mind like a half-finished melody, teasing him with their ambiguity. What was it he wasn't supposed to forget? And why had she written it for him?

It wasn't like him to get this caught up in a stranger. But something about her—her quiet confidence, the faint trace of sadness in her eyes—had unsettled him in a way he couldn't explain.

The next day, as if by some invisible pull, Jason found himself back at the café. He told himself it was for the coffee, but he knew better. The same table by the window was empty, her absence making the place feel oddly hollow.

Jason sighed and settled into his usual spot, trying to focus on his work. But his concentration fractured when the door chimed, and a familiar figure stepped inside.

It was her.

This time, she wasn't wearing the beret. Her hair fell loose around her shoulders, catching the afternoon light. She moved through the room with the same deliberate grace, but there was something different about her demeanor—more cautious, as if she were on edge.

Jason debated whether to approach her. The paper in his pocket felt like a burning question he was too afraid to ask.

She glanced around the café, her eyes grazing over him briefly before moving on. He wondered if she had recognized him, if she even remembered what she'd done the day before.

She sat at a table near the window, her notebook and pen appearing as if by magic. Jason's fingers hovered over his keyboard. The opportunity to speak to her felt like a door slowly closing, and if he didn't act now, it might never open again.

He stood, his palms slightly damp, and walked over. She looked up as he approached, her expression unreadable.

"Hi," Jason said, his voice a little unsteady. "I'm sorry to bother you, but..." He pulled the note from his pocket, holding it out to her. "You left this yesterday."

Her gaze dropped to the paper, her face betraying no reaction. Slowly, she took it from him, her fingers brushing his for the briefest moment.

"I know," she said softly, folding the note and tucking it into her coat pocket.

Jason blinked, caught off guard. "You know?"

She nodded, her lips curving into a faint smile. But it wasn't a reassuring smile. It was the kind that came with an unspoken warning, a shadow lurking just beneath the surface.

"Then why...?" He trailed off, unsure how to phrase the question that burned in his mind.

"Why did I leave it for you?" she finished for him. Her voice was calm, almost soothing, but it carried an edge that made Jason's pulse quicken. "I thought you might need it."

"Need it?" he echoed, baffled. "I don't even know what it means."

Her smile deepened, though her eyes remained distant. "Not yet, but you will."

Jason hesitated, his unease growing. "Look, if this is some kind of joke—"

"It's not a joke." Her tone turned sharper, cutting through his protest. "It's a reminder. For when you forget."

"Forget what?" Jason pressed.

Her gaze flickered, and for a moment, he thought he saw fear in her eyes. But she quickly masked it, shaking her head.

"You'll understand when the time comes," she said, rising to her feet.

Jason instinctively stepped back, startled by the abruptness of her movement. "Wait—what's your name?"

She paused, her hand resting lightly on the edge of the table. "Does it matter?"

"It does to me," he said firmly.

She studied him for a moment, as if weighing whether to answer. Finally, she sighed. "Eleanor," she said. "But you can call me Elle."

Before he could say anything else, she turned and walked out of the café, leaving him standing there with more questions than answers.

Jason watched her go, a sinking feeling settling in his chest. Something about this wasn't right.

And he was certain of one thing now—he wasn't just drawn to her. He was caught in something much bigger than himself.

# 3

## Letters Without Names

The first letter arrived three days after Jason last saw Elle.

He found it in the morning, tucked beneath the door of his apartment. No return address. No stamp. Just a plain envelope sealed with a single strip of tape.

Jason stared at it for a long moment before picking it up, his mind racing. Could it be from her? His fingers trembled slightly as he tore it open, pulling out a piece of thick, cream-colored paper.

The handwriting was instantly familiar—elegant and deliberate, just like the note she had left him in the café.

"When shadows fall and silence speaks,
   Remember the face that memory seeks.
   The path ahead is lined with thorns,
   But through the dark, a truth is born."

Jason read the poem twice, then a third time, but its meaning eluded him. His thoughts immediately jumped to Elle. It had to be from her. The handwriting matched, and the cryptic tone was unmistakable.

But why? What was she trying to tell him?

The unsettling realization crept over him—this wasn't just a coincidence. Elle hadn't entered his life by chance. She had chosen him for some reason, and now she was drawing him deeper into her web.

He tucked the letter back into its envelope, setting it on the kitchen counter. Part of him wanted to ignore it, to pretend it was some strange prank. But another part of him, the part that couldn't forget the way she had looked at him, knew he couldn't walk away.

The second letter came the next evening. This time, it was left on the windshield of his car.

Jason spotted it as he was leaving work, the corner of the envelope fluttering in the cold wind. His heart raced as he grabbed it, tearing it open right there in the parking lot.

"In the quiet of night, the answer will call,
  Through whispers that echo down shadowed halls.
  Beware the ones who watch and wait,
  For not all doors lead to fate."

Jason's breath caught. There was no doubt now—someone

was deliberately leaving these messages for him. And the line "Beware the ones who watch and wait" sent a shiver down his spine.

He glanced around the parking lot, his eyes scanning the rows of cars. But there was no one there. Just the dim glow of streetlights and the distant hum of traffic.

That night, Jason lay awake in his apartment, the letters spread out on the coffee table. He had read them so many times that the words were burned into his mind, but they still made no sense.

The following morning, the third letter appeared. This time, it was slid under his door like the first.

Jason hesitated before opening it, his nerves frayed. When he finally unfolded the paper, the message was even more chilling:

"The clock ticks loud when the past draws near,
    And the things you forget are what you should fear.
    Look to the place where memories hide,
    And find the truth that shadows divide."

Jason's chest tightened. The things you forget are what you should fear. The line felt like a direct challenge, as if Elle—or whoever was behind this—knew something he didn't.

He couldn't ignore it anymore. He had to find her.

Jason grabbed his phone and scrolled through his contacts. He had no number for Elle—she had never given him one. But he remembered where she had been sitting in the café and decided to start there.

The café was quiet when he arrived, the morning crowd already gone. Jason's eyes darted to the table by the window where Elle had been writing. It was empty now, but something felt off.

He approached the table cautiously, his pulse pounding. There, tucked beneath the salt shaker, was another letter.

Jason's hands shook as he opened it.

"When you met me, the story began.
   But every story has an end."

His knees nearly gave out. How long had this been planned? How could she have known he would come here?

Jason folded the letter carefully, his resolve hardening. Whoever Elle was, she wasn't just a stranger. She had pulled him into something far more dangerous than he had realized.

And he was determined to uncover the truth—no matter what it cost him.

# 4

## A Walk in the Mist

Jason stood at the edge of the park, staring into the soft veil of mist that seemed to blanket the world around him. It was late afternoon, and the fog had rolled in, thick and all-encompassing, muting the colors of the trees and the distant buildings. He'd come here on a whim, following the faintest pull in his gut. The letters had been growing darker, and the latest one had made something inside him snap—"Every story has an end." What end?

He scanned the park again, though he could barely see beyond a few feet in front of him. His thoughts raced back to Elle, to the way she had spoken to him with such calm certainty. It had been nearly a week since he last saw her, since that cold afternoon in the café. And yet, she was still haunting him with these letters, with her absence that felt like a presence all on its own.

"Jason."

The voice was barely audible through the mist, but it pierced through the fog like a knife. He turned sharply, his heart hammering in his chest.

She was standing there, no more than ten feet away, her figure barely distinguishable in the swirling white. Her coat flapped in the breeze, her eyes dark and unreadable.

Elle.

Jason's breath hitched, and he stepped toward her without thinking. "I didn't expect you to be here."

"Did you expect me anywhere else?" she asked, her voice tinged with amusement, though it felt forced, like she was hiding something.

He reached for her, a compulsion he couldn't understand driving him forward. "I've been looking for you. I—"

She held up her hand, stopping him. "Looking for answers, I know." Her eyes flickered around them, and she took a step back. "You shouldn't be here."

Jason frowned, confused. "Why? What is this place?"

Elle's gaze seemed to darken, and for a brief moment, she looked almost... haunted. She turned, starting to walk deeper into the park, her steps purposeful, as if she expected him to follow. Without a word, Jason obeyed, his instincts screaming at him to turn back, to question her, but he couldn't.

The fog grew heavier as they moved through the winding paths, the faint shapes of trees looming in the distance, their twisted branches almost like fingers reaching out from the shadows. The park was eerily quiet, save for the sound of their footsteps on the wet ground.

"Why the letters, Elle?" Jason asked, his voice low but urgent. "What is it you want me to understand?"

She didn't answer right away. Instead, she paused, looking out toward the center of the park. Her shoulders tensed, and Jason couldn't help but feel like they were being watched, as though the very mist around them held a thousand unseen eyes.

"Sometimes, you have to walk through the fog to find what's hidden," Elle said cryptically, almost to herself. "You don't even know what's waiting for you, Jason. But you'll find it soon enough."

Jason felt a chill run down his spine. "What do you mean? What's waiting?"

She turned to him suddenly, her gaze intense. "You're asking the wrong questions. The real question is—who are you running from?"

The words hit him like a physical blow. He froze, staring at her, his mind spinning. "What?"

Elle's lips curled into that same faint, unreadable smile. "The past isn't as far behind as you think. It's right there, waiting for you to remember."

Jason took a step back, his confusion mounting. "What do you mean by that? What's in the past? Who are you really?"

But she was already turning away again, continuing down the misty path, her voice barely audible over the wind. "There's a place here where all the answers lie. But not all of them should be found."

Jason hesitated. His feet felt heavy, reluctant to follow her deeper into the park. But he knew, in some part of him, that he couldn't stop now. Not when the words "all the answers lie" lingered in his mind like a challenge.

He caught up to her quickly, but when he reached her, she was standing in front of a large, wrought-iron gate. It was hidden behind overgrown ivy, barely noticeable against the backdrop of trees.

"What is this?" Jason asked, his voice barely more than a whisper.

Elle turned to face him, her eyes cold. "A place of endings and beginnings. You've been here before, Jason. You just don't know it."

The gate creaked as it swung open, revealing a narrow, twisting path that seemed to lead into darkness. Jason's heart raced in his chest as the hairs on the back of his neck stood up. He felt a deep, primal instinct telling him to turn away, to run, but he couldn't.

Without a word, Elle stepped into the darkness. Jason followed.

The air grew thicker the further they walked, the mist so dense now that it felt like they were moving through a wall. The path seemed to stretch on forever, and Jason's mind swirled with unanswered questions, but his legs felt like they were moving of their own accord.

Finally, the path opened into a small clearing, where an old stone bench sat beneath an overgrown oak tree. There, in the center of the clearing, was something Jason hadn't noticed before—a small, weathered box, half-buried beneath the dirt.

Elle stopped, her gaze fixed on the box. "This is where it all began."

Jason stared at the box, his pulse quickening. "What is it?"

Elle didn't answer. Instead, she crouched down, brushing the dirt away with her hands. Slowly, she opened the box.

Inside was a collection of old photographs, yellowed with age, and a small, folded note. Elle picked up the note and held it out to him, her fingers trembling slightly.

Jason took it, his heart pounding in his chest. He unfolded the note carefully, reading the single sentence written in the same elegant handwriting as the letters.

"The truth lies beneath the surface, but beware what you uncover."

Jason's hands shook as he stared at the words, the weight of them settling over him like a fog that refused to lift. He looked up at Elle, his voice hoarse. "What is this? What truth?"

Elle didn't answer. She simply turned and walked away, disappearing into the mist.

And as Jason stood there, staring at the box and the words that haunted him, he realized—he was already in too deep.

# 5

## The Edge of Memory

The days following his visit to the park felt like a blur. Jason had tried to shake the image of the old box, the cryptic note, and especially Elle's words from his mind. But they lingered, haunting him in the quiet moments, like a distant echo that grew louder with each passing day. The truth lies beneath the surface, but beware what you uncover.

Jason's sleep had become restless, filled with fractured dreams of mist-filled paths and unseen watchers. The same question looped endlessly in his mind: What was the truth? And more pressing—What was he forgetting?

He spent hours pouring over his past, retracing every detail of his life, looking for clues, signs—anything that could tie him to Elle. But every time he thought he was close to something, the memories slipped away, like water through his fingers.

That morning, he decided he had to confront her. He couldn't keep living in the shadows of his own mind. Something about

Elle, about the mystery she'd brought into his life, felt too dangerous to ignore.

Jason walked into the café, his nerves taut, the weight of his unanswered questions pressing down on him. The bell above the door jingled softly as he entered, and for a moment, the world seemed to hold its breath. He scanned the room.

There, in the far corner, sat Elle.

She was alone, a cup of coffee in front of her, her eyes focused on a notebook she was scribbling in. The same one from their first meeting, Jason noted with a flicker of recognition. The sight of her, so calmly lost in her writing, stirred something in him—an instinct, a need to understand.

He walked toward her, each step heavier than the last. She didn't look up until he was standing right beside her.

Her gaze met his, her lips curling into that same enigmatic smile that always left him questioning everything.

"Jason," she said, her voice as soft and smooth as velvet. "I didn't expect you to return so soon."

"Enough games, Elle," he said, his voice low but steady. "I need answers. Why have you been leaving me those letters? What is it you want from me?"

She tilted her head slightly, studying him with an expression he couldn't quite read. "Want from you?" she repeated, as if tasting the words on her tongue. "I don't want anything from you, Jason. But you—you want something, don't you? You want to know the truth."

Her words hit him like a slap, but there was something else in her tone—something softer, like a whispered warning.

"I do," he said, his hands gripping the edge of the table. "I want to understand what's happening. Why did you leave that note in the park? Why did you say I've been here before?"

Elle's eyes darkened, a flicker of something he couldn't name passing through them. She looked down at her notebook, then back at him, her lips pressed together in a thin line.

"You've been here before," she repeated, her voice barely above a whisper. "You just don't remember it yet."

Jason clenched his fists, frustration rising within him. "Stop speaking in riddles. If you know something about my past—about me—I need to know now."

Elle was silent for a long moment, her gaze fixed on him, unreadable. Then, finally, she spoke.

"You're not who you think you are, Jason. And neither am I."

The words landed in his chest with the force of a physical blow. His heart stuttered, and for a moment, the world seemed to tilt, the café blurring at the edges.

"What do you mean?" he managed, his voice cracking despite his effort to stay calm.

"I mean," Elle said, her voice steady now, "that everything you think you know about yourself is a lie. You're connected to this—to me—in ways you can't even begin to understand."

Jason felt the ground shift beneath him, his thoughts scrambling to keep up. A lie? What could she possibly mean? Was she talking about his past? His memories?

Elle's gaze softened, but there was still that unspoken warning in her eyes. "You've forgotten, Jason. And the more you remember, the more dangerous it becomes."

His mind raced, his pulse pounding in his ears. "Dangerous? What are you talking about? What do you want from me? Why are you doing this?"

Elle leaned forward slightly, her voice dropping to a whisper. "I'm not the one doing this to you. You are. Or rather—someone is. Someone who doesn't want you to remember."

Jason's breath caught. "Someone?" His throat tightened, the words feeling foreign on his tongue. "Who?"

But Elle didn't answer. Instead, she stood up abruptly, the chair scraping against the floor. She moved around the table, standing so close now that Jason could feel the warmth of her body, smell the faint trace of perfume in her hair.

Her lips brushed against his ear as she spoke, her words chilling him to the bone.

"Watch your back, Jason. They're closer than you think. And they won't stop until you forget everything."

Elle stepped away, her figure swallowed by the dim light of the café. Jason reached out instinctively, but she was already gone, vanishing into the crowd of people that had gathered at the counter.

Jason stood there, stunned, his thoughts spinning out of control. What had just happened? What was Elle trying to tell him?

He glanced around the café, his eyes searching for any sign of her, but she was nowhere to be found. The room had returned to its ordinary hum, the baristas chatting, the sounds of cups and saucers clinking. But the air felt heavier now, charged with something Jason couldn't shake.

With shaking hands, he pulled out his phone, his mind racing. Forget everything? What did that even mean? Was there something in his past that could explain all of this?

He scrolled through his contacts, stopping at the name of his therapist, Dr. Hayes. The only person he had confided in about his increasingly bizarre dreams.

He pressed the call button, waiting as the phone rang. When Dr. Hayes finally picked up, Jason's voice was shaky, urgent.

"I need to talk to you. Now."

# 6

## The Edge of Truth

Jason didn't sleep that night. Not really. He spent the hours tossing and turning in his bed, his mind too jumbled with questions to find rest. The last thing he remembered clearly was Elle's cryptic words echoing in his head, "Watch your back, Jason. They're closer than you think."

Who was they? What did she mean by that? What was she trying to tell him?

At sunrise, he could no longer stand the restless stirring in his chest. He grabbed his jacket and left the apartment, heading straight for Dr. Hayes' office.

Dr. Hayes was a no-nonsense, rational type of person, someone Jason had seen for the last few months in an attempt to make sense of the strange dreams he'd been having. But this... this was different. This was something beyond dreams, something far darker than anything he'd talked about in therapy before.

The moment Jason stepped into the office, he knew something was off. The air felt too still, the office too quiet. Dr. Hayes wasn't at his desk, the room empty except for a few of his books scattered across the floor.

"Dr. Hayes?" Jason called, his voice low, almost tentative. He stepped further into the room, a sense of unease growing in his stomach.

A sudden creak of the floorboards made him freeze. He turned quickly, his eyes scanning the room. But Dr. Hayes wasn't there.

Was anyone ever here?

Jason's pulse quickened. He approached the desk, noticing the glass of water sitting untouched, a paperweight that seemed slightly out of place. It wasn't like Dr. Hayes to leave his office in the middle of a session, especially when Jason had called ahead. The man had always been punctual, methodical, organized. But today, everything felt wrong.

He reached for the phone on the desk, dialing the number for Dr. Hayes' clinic. The phone rang, but there was no answer.

Jason's grip tightened on the receiver. The hairs on the back of his neck stood up. He placed the phone down gently, feeling a wave of tension ripple through him. Something wasn't right.

Then, he noticed it—the door to the back office was slightly ajar. The shadow of something—or someone—moved behind it.

Jason's heart pounded. He stood there, staring at the door, as though the darkness beyond it was somehow alive, breathing. He had a sudden, intense urge to flee, but something deeper compelled him forward.

With each step, the silence in the room seemed to grow heavier, more suffocating. His breath caught in his throat as he reached for the doorknob, turning it slowly, careful not to make a sound.

He pushed the door open, his eyes scanning the room.

Dr. Hayes' office looked the same as always. Neat, sterile. But something was different. The walls, the bookshelves—they all felt... off.

And then Jason saw it. The note.

It was placed carefully on the desk in front of the window. The handwriting was unmistakable: the same elegant script that had appeared in the letters Elle had been sending him.

Jason's stomach churned.

He walked over to the desk, his steps slow and deliberate. His fingers hesitated just above the paper, and then, with a deep breath, he unfolded it.

"The past can only be forgotten for so long, Jason. It's always been you, but you've been blind to it. Now, the truth will find you, whether you're ready or not."

Jason's vision blurred for a moment, and he had to steady himself against the desk. His mind was spinning—what did this mean? How was Dr. Hayes connected to any of this? What was the truth?

Before he could think any further, a sudden sound from behind him made him freeze.

A soft thud, like the sound of a door closing. He whirled around, his pulse racing, but there was nothing. No one. Just the dim light filtering in from the windows.

"Jason..."

The voice came from the far corner of the room, low and calm, yet somehow suffused with a chilling authority.

He turned, his breath caught in his throat. There, standing in the shadowed corner, was Dr. Hayes.

But the man he saw was not the same calm, composed therapist Jason had known. His face was pale, his eyes dark, hollow. There was something... wrong with him. Something terrifying.

Dr. Hayes stepped forward, his movements slow and deliberate, as if he were carefully measuring each step.

"I see you've found my note," he said, his voice flat, lacking the warmth Jason had once come to expect. "Good. You're starting to understand now."

Jason stumbled back, his thoughts racing. "What the hell is going on? Who are you? What have you done?"

Dr. Hayes chuckled softly, a sound that sent a chill straight down Jason's spine. "I've done nothing but help you see the truth, Jason. You've just been too blind to understand it."

Jason took another step back, his heart pounding. "What truth? I don't understand!"

Dr. Hayes smiled—a twisted, cold smile that made Jason's blood run cold. "The truth you've been running from your entire life. The truth about your past, about Elle. Everything you think you know is a lie."

Jason's stomach churned, his body suddenly overwhelmed with the desire to escape. But Dr. Hayes was standing between him and the door now, blocking the way out.

"Why?" Jason managed, his voice trembling. "Why didn't you tell me? What's the connection between me and her?"

Dr. Hayes didn't answer immediately. Instead, he took a step forward, his gaze fixed on Jason, and for the first time, Jason saw something in the man's eyes—a flicker of something darker.

"You think you're in control of your life," Dr. Hayes said softly. "But you're not. Not anymore."

Jason's breath caught in his chest. "What are you talking about?"

"The past is catching up with you, Jason. And you're not going to be able to outrun it."

Before Jason could react, the lights in the office flickered, plunging them into darkness. The sudden loss of light made the air feel thick, oppressive. Jason's heart hammered in his chest, the darkness closing in on him. He could hear Dr. Hayes' footsteps moving closer, and he felt the cold, oppressive weight of the man's presence pressing down on him.

"Jason," Dr. Hayes' voice whispered, barely audible in the suffocating dark. "It's time to remember."

And then, everything went black.

# 7

# The Shattered Reflection

*Jason awoke with a start, gasping for breath as if he had been underwater. His body trembled, his heart still hammering in his chest, as though the terror of his dream—or was it a nightmare?—had seeped into his very soul. He sat up in the darkness, disoriented, unsure of where he was. His head throbbed, as if the weight of his thoughts had physically taken their toll.*

It took him a few moments to realize he was no longer in Dr. Hayes' office. He was lying on the cold floor of his own apartment, the dim light of the early morning creeping through the blinds. He couldn't remember how he got here. The last thing he remembered was the darkness—the oppressive weight of Dr. Hayes' presence, the suffocating silence—and then, nothing.

Was it a dream? Had it all been a dream?

Jason rubbed his temples, trying to calm the disorienting fog that clouded his mind. He could still feel the lingering presence of Dr. Hayes, hear his words: *"It's time to remember."* What had he meant by that?

Shaking, Jason stood up, his body unsteady as he made his way to the bathroom. The harsh fluorescent light above flickered as he turned the faucet, splashing cold water on his face. As he stared into the mirror, he saw his reflection—his eyes wild, his hair disheveled, and a look of desperation written across his face.

He froze.

There, beneath his reflection, something shifted.

The face staring back at him was still his, but there was something *off* about it. For a brief moment, his reflection seemed to waver—an almost imperceptible distortion, like the surface of water rippling with unseen waves. His eyes blinked, but his reflection didn't. It stared back at him, unblinking, with a coldness he couldn't explain.

Jason's breath hitched, and he stepped back from the mirror, his pulse quickening. He felt an overwhelming urge to turn away, but his gaze was locked. He couldn't look away. It was as if the reflection held some secret he needed to uncover, some truth he wasn't prepared to face.

*"It's time to remember."*

The words rang in his ears again, as if they were being spoken directly into his mind. He reached out, his hand trembling as he touched the glass. The cold surface sent a shock through his fingertips, but he didn't pull away.

And then, in a blink, the reflection changed.

His image cracked—like a shattered piece of glass—and the figure in the mirror was no longer his own. It was Elle.

Jason stumbled back, his heart pounding in his chest. His mind raced. What was happening? Why was she in the mirror?

Elle's face was pale, her expression unreadable, just as it had been when they last met. But now, her eyes seemed *different*—darker, almost... *empty*. There was no warmth in them, only an abyss.

For a moment, Jason wondered if he was losing his grip on reality. Was this some kind of hallucination? Was the stress of everything—Elle, the letters, Dr. Hayes—finally taking its toll?

But as he continued to stare, something strange began to unfold in the reflection. Elle's face didn't remain still. It morphed, twisted, her features warping and distorting like a melting painting. The image flickered between Elle's face and his own, back and forth, as though both were fighting for dominance.

*"You're not who you think you are,"* her voice echoed in the room, though her lips never moved.

Jason's head swam. He reached for his phone, fumbling to unlock it with shaking hands. His thoughts were spiraling, each new revelation deeper than the last. He needed to talk to someone—anyone—someone who could make sense of this madness.

He scrolled through his contacts, his fingers trembling, until he found the name he was looking for. It wasn't Dr. Hayes—he couldn't go back there, not after everything. Instead, he dialed a number he hadn't thought about in a long time.

Elle.

The phone rang, the sound filling the silence in the room like a death knell. The seconds felt like minutes. And then, to his surprise, the call went through.

"Jason," Elle's voice answered on the other end, calm and steady, as if everything was perfectly normal.

"Elle," he gasped, his voice ragged. "What's happening? What is this? Why did you—why are you in my reflection? Why—"

She interrupted him, her tone almost soft, almost gentle. "Jason, you need to stop looking for answers. Some things are better left unknown."

"Unknown?" Jason repeated, his voice cracking with frustration. "You've been leaving me these letters, giving me riddles, telling me to remember, and now *this*—my reflection changing, you—"

Elle's voice grew colder. "Stop. It's already started, and there's no turning back."

Jason felt his heart stop at her words. "What do you mean? What's started?"

There was a long pause on the other end of the line. Then, quietly, Elle spoke again, her voice barely above a whisper. "It was always meant to be this way. Don't you see? The past is waking up."

Jason froze, his mind struggling to grasp what she was saying. "The past? What does that mean? Who *am* I?"

"You're not ready for the truth yet," Elle replied, her voice distant now, as if she were already walking away. "But soon, Jason... soon, you will be."

And with that, the line went dead.

Jason stood there, holding the phone to his ear, his mind in turmoil. He felt as though the floor had dropped out from under him, and he was left suspended in an abyss of uncertainty. What had just happened? What did Elle mean by "the past is waking up"?

The reflection in the bathroom mirror flashed in his mind again—the distorted face, the coldness of Elle's eyes. He had to know what was happening. He couldn't let it go.

But as Jason stood there, staring at his phone, a strange sensation washed over him. The world around him seemed to shift, subtly at first, like a slight distortion at the edges of his vision. The air felt heavier, charged with an energy that he couldn't quite place.

A noise interrupted his thoughts—a knock at the door.

Jason's heart skipped a beat.

Who could it be? He hadn't invited anyone over. And yet, there was no mistaking the sound—a sharp, insistent knock, repeated again.

He hesitated. His hand hovered over the doorknob, and as his fingers brushed against it, the door suddenly burst open.

Standing in the doorway was Dr. Hayes.

But this was not the same man who had sat across from him in the office. This man was different—his eyes were hollow, his movements jerky, unnatural. And in his hand, he held something small and black, like a compact mirror.

Jason's blood ran cold.

"*It's time to remember,*" Dr. Hayes said, his voice flat, emotionless.

# 8

## The Weight of the Truth

Jason stood frozen at the threshold of his apartment, his eyes locked on Dr. Hayes. The man's presence in his doorway felt like an intrusion—alien, yet somehow inevitable. His fingers trembled against the doorframe, his thoughts racing as he tried to make sense of what was happening.

"You shouldn't have come here," Jason muttered, his voice shaking with a mixture of fear and defiance. "I don't know what you want, but I—"

"You don't know anything, Jason." Dr. Hayes interrupted, his voice too calm, too cold. There was no warmth in his words, just an unshakable certainty that made Jason's blood run cold. "That's the problem, isn't it? You think you know what's happening. But the truth is so much darker than you can possibly imagine."

Jason's pulse hammered in his throat as he backed away from the door. He wanted to shut it, to escape, but something stopped him. The strange energy that had filled the room ever since Elle's call had only intensified. It pressed in on him, thick and suffocating, as if the very air was charged with something unspeakable.

"What do you want from me?" Jason demanded, his voice louder now. He took another step back, but Dr. Hayes followed, moving with a strange, predatory grace. His eyes were locked on Jason's, unblinking, as if he were measuring every thought, every movement.

"I want you to understand, Jason," Dr. Hayes said, his voice almost a whisper. "I want you to finally understand the game you've been a part of. The game you've been running from, but can never escape."

Jason's head spun. A game? He had no idea what Dr. Hayes was talking about, but every instinct screamed at him to run, to break free of this nightmare. But his legs felt like lead, his body rooted to the spot as though the room itself was holding him captive.

"You've been chasing shadows, Jason," Dr. Hayes continued, stepping closer, his face now inches from Jason's. "Every step you've taken, every choice you've made, has been leading you here. You're part of something much bigger than you realize."

Jason swallowed, trying to steady his breath. "You're insane," he whispered, almost to himself. "This isn't real. None of this makes sense." He stepped back again, his eyes darting around the room, looking for an escape—any way out. But the door remained wide open, and the hallway outside was empty.

"Oh, it's real, Jason," Dr. Hayes said, a twisted smile curling on his lips. "It's as real as your past. You've just been too afraid to face it. Too afraid to see what's been staring you in the face the whole time."

The words hit Jason like a punch to the gut. His mind spun in circles, trying to piece together the fragments of memories that were still so unclear. His past—what did Dr. Hayes know about his past? What was he hiding?

"You've been looking for answers, but you haven't been asking the right questions," Dr. Hayes said. "The truth about Elle, about you... it's all connected. But you've been blind to it. You've been running from it."

Jason's throat tightened, the weight of the man's words pressing down on him like a vice. "No," he managed to say, his voice barely a whisper. "I don't believe you. You're lying."

Dr. Hayes' expression hardened, the smile fading into something colder, more calculating. "You still don't get it, do you, Jason? You think you're the one in control here. But the truth is, you're just a pawn in someone else's game. You've always been a pawn."

A chill ran through Jason's spine as the room seemed to darken, the shadows growing longer, more oppressive. He stepped backward again, his mind racing with a thousand questions, but no answers. How could this be happening? How had his life gotten so tangled up in these impossible threads?

"You're not alone in this, Jason," Dr. Hayes said, his voice suddenly softer, almost coaxing. "Elle was never just a girl. She was part of the plan, too. You and her... your destinies were tied long before you ever met. You're both pieces in something much larger. The question is: are you ready to face what you've been running from all these years?"

Jason's head spun, his chest tightening as though he couldn't breathe. The words didn't make sense—destinies tied? A plan? What was Dr. Hayes saying? What was happening to him?

Suddenly, the air in the room felt heavy with something unspoken, like the silence before a storm. Jason's gaze fell to the floor, where Dr. Hayes had placed the black compact mirror. It was open, the reflective surface catching the dim light. Jason didn't want to look at it, but something in the pit of his stomach told him that he needed to.

He reached out, his fingers trembling as they brushed the cool glass. As soon as he touched it, a flood of memories hit him—too fast, too vivid. His heart raced as images of his childhood, his family, and moments from his life he had long since buried surfaced in a chaotic rush. He saw faces—faces of people he didn't recognize, yet somehow knew. He saw a younger version of himself, looking lost, confused, and a woman... a woman with the same dark, empty eyes that he had seen in Elle's reflection.

Jason staggered back, his hand falling away from the mirror. The flood of memories ceased as abruptly as it had come, leaving him gasping for breath, clutching his chest as though he had just been plunged underwater.

"What was that?" he gasped, his voice a mix of disbelief and terror. "What did you do to me?"

Dr. Hayes stood motionless, his expression unreadable. "I didn't do anything to you, Jason. I only showed you what you've been trying to forget. What you've been running from your entire life."

Jason felt a knot tighten in his stomach as he realized the truth—the truth that had been lurking beneath the surface all this time, just beyond his reach. His entire life had been a lie. The memories, the people, the pieces that never quite fit—they were all part of a puzzle he hadn't known how to solve. And now, it was too late to turn back.

"You need to decide," Dr. Hayes said, his voice low and almost sympathetic. "Do you want to keep pretending? Keep running from what you are, from who you really are? Or will you face the truth? The truth about who you've always been… and the role you're meant to play in what's coming next?"

Jason's heart raced. He wanted to scream, to shout, to demand answers, but the words caught in his throat. The weight of the truth pressed down on him, crushing the air from his lungs. How could he ever face the truth now? How could he ever be the same?

But before he could answer, before he could even form another thought, a sudden, piercing noise split the air—the sound of something shattering, like glass breaking into a thousand pieces. Jason spun toward the window.

A figure stood there in the street below, silhouetted against the distant glow of the streetlights.

Elle.

She was looking up at him, her face emotionless, as if waiting for something. Waiting for him.

And then, without a word, she turned and vanished into the shadows.

# 9

## The Echo of the Unseen

Jason's heart pounded in his chest as he stood at the window, his eyes locked on the empty street below. The figure that had been standing there—Elle—was gone. But the eerie sensation that lingered in the air told him she hadn't just vanished. Something deeper, something far more unsettling, had shifted.

His mind raced, swirling with the events of the last few days— his encounter with Dr. Hayes, the strange mirror, the chilling words that had been whispered in his ear. Everything felt like a thread, each moment pulling him deeper into a web he couldn't escape. His feet felt heavy, and the walls of his apartment seemed to close in around him.

Jason backed away from the window, his pulse still racing, as if the very air around him had thickened with danger. He glanced at the black mirror still sitting on the floor, its reflective surface dark and ominous. It felt like a trap, a thing that had been waiting for him to make a mistake, waiting for him to finally give in to whatever was pulling him closer to the truth. But what was the truth? What had Elle meant by all those cryptic words? And what was Dr. Hayes' role in all of this?

His thoughts were interrupted by the sudden ringing of his phone.

Jason hesitated before picking it up, the sense of dread mounting in his chest. He knew who it would be, and yet he couldn't bring himself to ignore it. He pressed the phone to his ear, his throat tight.

"Jason," came Elle's voice, soft but unmistakable. "You're running out of time."

The words made his skin crawl, as if they were meant to sink into his bones, to take root and grow there. His breath caught, and he leaned against the wall for support.

"What do you want from me?" Jason asked, his voice trembling, though he tried to sound steady. "I don't understand. Why—why is this happening?"

Elle's laugh echoed through the phone, a sound that was almost hollow, empty. "You've been asking the wrong questions, Jason. The answers are already inside you. You've always known, but you've refused to see."

Jason gritted his teeth. "Stop talking in riddles. Tell me what's going on. What's happening to me?"

There was a long pause on the other end, and when she spoke

again, her voice was quieter, more distant. "You're not alone in this. You never have been. You've been a part of something much bigger than yourself, something that's been waiting for the right moment to awaken."

"What are you talking about?" Jason's voice cracked as the weight of her words pressed down on him, like an anchor pulling him into a black, endless sea.

"Everything is connected," Elle whispered, and Jason could hear the faint sound of her breathing, as if she were in the room with him. "The past, the present... they're merging, Jason. And when the past comes for you, there's no place to hide."

The line went dead.

Jason's grip on the phone tightened, his knuckles white. He stood in the middle of the room, the words reverberating in his mind like a drumbeat: No place to hide. He felt the floor beneath him shift, a sensation as though the world was tilting slightly, throwing him off balance. The apartment felt too small now, as if the walls were pressing in, suffocating him with the weight of everything he didn't understand.

The mirror. He couldn't ignore it anymore. The black mirror. It seemed to call to him, beckoning him like a whisper from the void. What did it mean? What was it showing him?

Jason took a deep breath, his hands shaking as he reached down and picked it up. The glass felt cold against his fingers, sending a jolt through his arm. He held it in front of him, staring at the reflection that stared back.

For a moment, it was just his face, his own weary eyes staring back at him. But then, just as before, the reflection began to shift. Slowly, it changed, morphing like liquid under the pressure of an unseen force. The face in the mirror blurred and wavered, and Jason's breath caught in his throat as he watched it transform—first into Elle's face, and then back to his own, but different, distorted. The reflection was wrong. The features didn't match up, the angles of his face too sharp, the eyes too dark.

No, no, no...

Jason stumbled back, his heart racing in his chest. He dropped the mirror onto the floor, the shattering sound ringing through the silence of the room. He didn't want to look. He couldn't bear to look, but his eyes were drawn to it, to the fragments of glass now scattered across the floor. The pieces of the mirror reflected shards of his own image, but something was wrong. The reflections in the broken glass didn't match the reality in front of him. They were darker, distorted, twisted.

As he stood frozen, unable to tear his gaze away from the shattered pieces, a soft whisper filled the room, as if coming from the mirror itself, from the reflections lying broken on the floor.

"You're still not ready."

Jason's breath caught in his throat, the voice echoing through his mind as if it were a memory he hadn't yet uncovered. It sounded like Elle's voice—but distorted, hollow, like it was coming from far away.

He looked around the apartment, feeling the air thicken around him. He could hear the faintest of sounds—footsteps, barely audible, coming from the hallway outside. Jason's pulse spiked again, and he felt a chill crawl up his spine. It wasn't just the phone call, the mirror, or even Dr. Hayes' cryptic words. There was something else now. Someone else. Something was moving in the apartment with him.

His heart hammered against his ribs as he crept toward the door, moving slowly, cautiously. His hand hovered over the doorknob, and for a moment, he considered leaving. He considered running—running far away, as fast as he could, until the questions, the fear, the shadows were behind him.

But before he could make a move, the footsteps grew louder. They were getting closer. Jason's breath quickened, his hand shaking as he gripped the doorknob and yanked the door open.

Nothing.

There was nothing in the hallway. No one there.

He stepped into the hallway, his eyes scanning the empty space. His heart pounded in his chest as the silence pressed in on him, suffocating. Every step felt like it was pulling him deeper into the unknown.

Then, he heard it again. A soft whisper—almost a laugh—coming from behind him.

Jason spun around, his chest tight, but the hallway remained empty.

But this time, he saw something that made his blood run cold. A figure standing at the end of the corridor. Tall, shadowed, unmoving. It wasn't Elle. It wasn't Dr. Hayes.

It was a person. A stranger. A face he didn't recognize, but somehow, in the depth of his gut, he knew this person had been waiting for him.

The figure took a step forward.

Jason's breath caught, his body frozen in place, as he realized—whatever this was, it was no longer just about him. The past, the present, the people he didn't remember—everything was converging.

And there was no escape.

"It's time," the figure whispered.

Jason turned and ran.

# 10

## Into the Shadows

Jason's footsteps pounded against the cold, polished floor as he sprinted down the hallway, the sound of his breathing frantic in his ears. His mind was a whirl of confusion and terror, racing to make sense of everything that had happened. That figure—standing in the shadows at the end of the corridor—had felt like a premonition, a warning of something he wasn't ready for, something that had been waiting for him.

But there was no time to process it. No time to think.

He reached the staircase and barreled down it, the walls around him blurring as he descended, every muscle in his body screaming at him to keep moving. He had to get out. Get away from the apartment, away from everything. The echoes of footsteps following him, so close now that he could hear them too clearly, only pushed him harder, faster. They were gaining on him.

His breath was coming in ragged bursts, the panic starting to set in as his legs burned with the effort. He reached the bottom of the stairs, barely taking a breath before throwing open the door and stumbling into the street.

The cold night air hit him like a slap in the face, sharp and biting. But it was no relief. The sensation of being watched, of being hunted, clung to him, wrapping around him like an invisible net. His eyes darted frantically around the street. No one. No one was there. The city stretched out before him, quiet, indifferent, but the feeling of unease wasn't fading. It was growing.

Jason's heart was still pounding in his chest as he glanced back over his shoulder. He half-expected to see the figure there, in the doorway, emerging from the shadows with slow, deliberate steps. But nothing. The street behind him was empty. Still. Silent.

He kept moving, though, faster now, not daring to stop, not daring to look back again. His body was on autopilot, carrying him through the darkened streets without thought. It was almost as though something outside of himself was guiding him, pushing him forward. The world around him felt unreal—distant, hazy, as if he were walking through a dream, but one filled with too much dread. Too much fear.

He didn't know where he was going. He just knew he had to keep moving.

Then, a voice—low, gravelly, like it came from the very pit of the earth—broke through the silence.

"You can't outrun it, Jason."

Jason froze, his blood running cold at the sound. The voice had come from behind him, from somewhere just outside his field of vision. His pulse spiked, his skin prickling as he slowly turned around.

There, standing at the corner of the street, was Dr. Hayes. His figure emerged from the darkness as though he had been waiting for Jason all along. His eyes glinted in the dim light of the streetlamps, gleaming with an unsettling calmness.

"I told you, didn't I?" Dr. Hayes said, his voice soft, almost soothing. "You can't escape what you are. What's coming for you. It's been waiting for so long. And now, Jason… you've finally crossed the threshold."

Jason's body stiffened, every instinct telling him to run. He couldn't stay here. He couldn't be close to this man. Not after everything that had happened. But his legs wouldn't move. He felt paralyzed, caught in Dr. Hayes' gaze, his mind spinning with questions and fear.

"What do you want from me?" Jason demanded, trying to keep his voice steady despite the rising terror in his chest. "Why are you following me? Why won't you leave me alone?"

Dr. Hayes smiled, the expression devoid of warmth. "You think you have a choice? You think you can still run from this?" He took a step forward, and Jason instinctively stepped back. "You've already made your choice, Jason. And now it's time to face the consequences."

Jason's heart raced in his chest, each beat a frantic reminder that there was something more to this—something that was beyond his control. "I don't know what you're talking about," he said, his voice hoarse. "I don't know who you are. What is this? What are you doing to me?"

Dr. Hayes tilted his head, his smile turning cruel. "You've always known. You just refused to see it. All of it—the dreams, the memories, the strange feeling that something was wrong in your life. It was never a coincidence, Jason. It was never a random sequence of events. Everything is connected. And now you've finally stepped into the center of it. The truth has come for you."

Jason felt a chill wash over him, something colder than the night air around him, colder than the dread that had been building in his chest. His throat tightened. He had been right all along, hadn't he? There was something—something lurking beneath the surface of his life, something he had been running from, refusing to confront. But now, it was here. It had found him.

"What do you want?" Jason repeated, his voice barely a whisper, as if speaking too loudly would shatter whatever fragile thread of control he still had left.

"I want you to understand, Jason," Dr. Hayes said, stepping closer, his eyes never leaving Jason's. "I want you to see the truth. To understand the part you've been playing all along."

Jason's breath hitched. Part? He didn't understand. Nothing made sense anymore. How could he have been playing a part?

He had been a normal guy, a guy just trying to get through life without being swept up in the chaos. He never asked for this. He never asked for any of it.

But Dr. Hayes wasn't waiting for an answer. He didn't need to. "Everything you've known, everything you've believed... it was all a lie," Dr. Hayes continued. "The memories, the people, even Elle. They've all been part of something bigger. Something you've been a part of from the very beginning."

Jason's head spun. Elle? She was part of this too? She was the key to it, the reason this madness was happening. But how? What role had she played in all of this?

Before Jason could ask, a distant sound broke through the tension—a hum, soft at first, but growing louder. It sounded like an engine, like a car revving in the distance. Jason's head snapped to the side, his eyes narrowing as he tried to locate the source of the noise.

And then, from around the corner, a car appeared. It was sleek, black, and moving faster than it should have been, like it was coming straight for him.

Dr. Hayes stepped back, a knowing look crossing his face. "Your past is coming for you, Jason," he said softly. "You can't run from it anymore. You can't hide from it."

Jason's body tensed as the car grew closer. It was moving fast—too fast—and Jason's mind screamed at him to move, to get out of the way. But he couldn't. His legs felt rooted to the ground.

The car screeched to a halt in front of him, the headlights blinding him for a moment. The door swung open, and a figure stepped out. The figure's silhouette was obscured by the darkness, but Jason knew, somehow, that this was the moment.

This was the moment everything would change.

The figure stepped into the light, and Jason's breath caught in his throat.

It was Elle.

Her eyes locked with his, and for a moment, neither of them moved. The world around them seemed to stand still, as if everything had been leading to this moment. The silence between them was suffocating, the air thick with unspoken words and memories that Jason couldn't quite place.

But then Elle spoke, her voice a mere whisper that cut through the tension.

"It's time to go, Jason," she said, her eyes flickering with something darker, something Jason couldn't understand. "The past is waiting."

Before he could react, before he could say a word, she turned and walked toward the car.

Jason's feet finally moved, his mind still reeling from the revelation, the fear gnawing at him like a hungry beast. He had no choice. There was nowhere else to go.

But as he took a step toward her, he couldn't shake the feeling that he was about to step into the unknown, into something he could never escape. The shadows were closing in, and Jason was about to be consumed by them.

# 11

## The Secrets Beneath

The car sped through the city streets, its tires cutting through the night like a knife through silk. Jason sat in the backseat, his eyes glued to the darkened streets outside, the flashing streetlights giving fleeting glimpses of the world beyond. Elle sat beside him, her presence both comforting and unsettling at the same time. There was something in her eyes, something that wasn't quite right, and yet he couldn't look away. She hadn't said a word since she opened the car door, but the silence between them was thick, laden with unsaid things.

Jason shifted uncomfortably in his seat, his hands clenched tight at his sides. His mind was still reeling from the events of the past few hours—Dr. Hayes' cryptic words, the encounter with the figure in the shadows, and now Elle, whose very presence seemed to be unraveling the fragile grip he had on his reality. He had to know more. He had to understand what was going on, or he might lose himself entirely.

"Where are we going?" Jason finally broke the silence, his voice strained, barely above a whisper.

Elle didn't turn to look at him. She just stared ahead, her face unreadable in the dim glow of the dashboard lights. Her lips parted slightly, but she didn't speak at first.

"It's not about where we're going, Jason," she said softly, her voice distant, almost as if she were speaking to herself. "It's about where you've already been."

Jason's chest tightened, a shiver running down his spine. "What are you talking about? I don't understand. I need answers. What happened back at the apartment? What was Dr. Hayes trying to tell me?"

Elle's fingers tapped lightly against the edge of the seat. She didn't look at him, but her voice grew colder, harder. "You've been running from the truth, Jason. From all of it. But the truth has a way of finding you, no matter how far you run. And now... now you have no choice but to face it."

Jason's thoughts spiraled. Running from the truth? No choice? What was she talking about? He felt as if he were on the edge of something, something vast and incomprehensible, and every moment he spent with her, the closer he was to falling into it.

"Elle..." he started, but she raised her hand, silencing him before he could say more.

"Shh..." she whispered, her voice barely audible. "It's time."

Jason frowned, but before he could ask what she meant, the car abruptly turned off the main road, onto a narrow, unlit street. The lights outside flickered and dimmed as the car's engine hummed steadily beneath them. The further they drove, the more isolated they became, the buildings narrowing and the streets darker, until Jason could hardly make out any features in the surroundings. It felt like they were leaving the city behind, entering some other place entirely—a place outside of time, outside of everything he knew.

The silence stretched between them once again, but this time it was different. There was something suffocating about it, something ancient and pressing. Jason glanced at Elle, but her face was shadowed, her expression unreadable.

Finally, the car slowed, pulling into a small, overgrown lot at the end of the street. The headlights cut through the darkness, illuminating a dilapidated, weather-beaten building. The structure loomed in the night like a forgotten monument, its windows dark and shattered, the air around it thick with neglect.

Jason's stomach churned as the car came to a stop. He couldn't understand what he was feeling—something cold, something foreign, like the air itself was warning him not to go any further. The hairs on the back of his neck stood on end.

Elle opened the door and stepped out, her movements fluid and purposeful. She didn't wait for Jason. She simply started walking toward the building, her back straight, her pace deliberate. Jason hesitated, torn between following her and running back to the car, back to the safety of the unknown. But deep down, he knew he had no choice. He had come this far.

With a deep breath, Jason opened the door and followed her.

The air around him felt heavier as he stepped out of the car, the darkness pressing in from all sides. The building seemed to swallow the sound of his footsteps, the only noise his own breath, ragged and uneven as he approached the entrance. He glanced at Elle, who was already at the door, waiting for him.

"Are you sure about this?" he asked, his voice almost a whisper, the fear choking him. "What is this place? What's inside?"

Elle turned to face him, her eyes searching his face with an intensity that made his chest tighten. "This is where it begins. Where it all started. The place where you'll finally remember."

Jason's heart skipped a beat. "Remember what?"

But Elle didn't answer. She turned and stepped inside, the creak of the door echoing into the silence. Jason stood frozen for a moment, the darkness surrounding him like a living thing, before he followed her.

The interior of the building was dim, lit only by the faint light of a few flickering bulbs hanging from the ceiling. The air was stale, thick with the smell of dust and something else—something metallic, like blood. Jason's gaze darted around the room, taking in the rusted metal fixtures, the worn, cracked floorboards, and the long-abandoned furniture that sat in the corners like forgotten relics.

Elle was already moving deeper into the building, her steps sure and unhesitating. Jason hurried to catch up, his mind a tangled mess of questions and dread.

They reached the end of a long hallway, and Elle stopped in front of a large wooden door. The door was old, the wood cracked and weathered, as if it had been here for centuries. There was something about it, something that felt wrong. A chill ran down Jason's spine as he looked at the door, the feeling in his gut growing stronger, more insistent.

"This is it," Elle said, her voice barely a whisper. "This is where the truth lies."

Jason stood there, frozen, his pulse pounding in his ears. He felt as if he were standing on the edge of a cliff, looking down into an abyss that would swallow him whole. He couldn't go back. He couldn't escape. There was nowhere left to run.

With a deep breath, Jason stepped forward. His hand reached for the door handle, his fingers trembling as he wrapped them around it. The metal was cold, unforgiving beneath his touch. Slowly, carefully, he turned the handle, and the door creaked open.

Inside, the room was pitch-black, the air heavy with an unseen presence. Jason stepped inside, his heart hammering, his eyes straining to make out anything in the dark.

And then, the light flickered on.

The walls of the room were lined with mirrors. Dozens of mirrors, each one cracked, shattered, or tarnished in some way. And at the center of the room, there was a large mirror—untouched, pristine, its surface glowing faintly in the dim light.

Elle stood behind him now, silent, watching.

Jason moved toward the mirror, his breath shallow. He could feel something pulling him in, like gravity, something undeniable, something that was both terrifying and irresistible. He reached out a hand, his fingers trembling as they neared the surface.

And then, the reflection shifted.

Jason gasped, stumbling backward as the mirror seemed to change, as if it were no longer reflecting just him, but something else. Something darker. The face in the mirror—his face—twisted, its features distorting as if the mirror were alive, breathing.

The room began to spin around him, the walls closing in, the mirrors reflecting a thousand different versions of himself, all of them wrong, all of them shifting and warping into something grotesque.

"No," he whispered, backing away from the mirror. "No, this can't be—"

Elle's voice echoed in the darkness. "You've always known, Jason. The truth was inside you all along. And now... you see it."

The room around him spun faster, the mirrors flashing images of a past he didn't remember—flashes of faces, of places, of names he had never known.

And then, as if the world had cracked open, Jason understood.

The truth. The truth was worse than he could have ever imagined. And it was more dangerous than anything he had ever feared.

The darkness was coming for him. And he was powerless to stop it.

## 12

## Fractured Memories

Jason's breath came in short, ragged gasps, the air thick with tension and suffocating dread. He staggered backward, his heart hammering in his chest, as his reflection in the mirror warped before his eyes. The crackling air around him seemed to pulse, alive with something unexplainable, something beyond the physical. His mind reeled, struggling to make sense of the dark maze of images flashing through his mind.

He could feel Elle's gaze burning into his back, cold and distant, as though she were watching a stranger—a stranger who was unraveling before her eyes.

The mirrors around the room seemed to stretch, their glass surfaces undulating as if they were alive, each one flickering with images of his past—his childhood, faces he didn't recognize, moments he had never lived. A fleeting moment in a forest, a bloodied hand reaching for him, a whisper from a woman's voice, too distant to understand.

Jason's head throbbed with the onslaught of memories, memories that didn't belong to him, memories that felt as though they were being forced into his mind. He could hear the faint echo of voices, too soft, too distorted to make out.

No, no, this can't be real. These aren't my memories.

He clenched his fists, desperately trying to ground himself, to separate what was his from what was being fed into his mind. But every time he closed his eyes, the images grew stronger, clearer. A woman with dark eyes, her face shadowed in grief. A child—his child?—reaching for him, their tiny hand outstretched, trembling. A man in the shadows, always watching, always waiting.

His head spun, the disorientation mounting with each passing second.

"Jason," Elle's voice cut through the fog of his thoughts. It was calm, but there was something sharp, like a knife scraping against glass. "It's time."

He whirled toward her, his hands shaking. "What is this? What's happening to me?"

She was standing just inside the doorway now, her silhouette sharp against the dim light. Her face remained impassive, almost too composed, but there was something in her eyes—something too deep, too knowing—that made Jason's stomach churn.

"It's happening because you're finally ready," Elle replied, her voice low and steady, like she was speaking to a child. "You've been running, hiding from what you are, from what you've always been."

Jason's pulse raced. The truth she spoke was like a heavy weight pressing against his chest, suffocating him. He didn't know what she meant. He didn't know what he was, or what he had been running from.

He took a step forward, his hand reaching out as if to touch her, but then something—no—someone—stopped him. A shadow moved at the edge of his vision, flickering in and out of sight, but always there. The shadow of a man. The figure from his dreams.

Jason's breath caught in his throat, his pulse spiking.

"Who is that?" he whispered, his voice hoarse. "Who is he?"

Elle didn't answer immediately. Instead, she gave him a long, silent look, as though weighing the gravity of what she was about to say. Then, in a voice so quiet it was almost a whisper, she said, "He's your past, Jason. He's the part of you that's been buried. The part you've been trying to forget."

Jason's chest tightened. He felt the ground beneath him shift, as if the very room were sinking, pulling him deeper into a void. His hand hovered near his head, his fingers running through his hair in agitation. He could feel it—everything he had forgotten was clawing its way back to the surface.

The memories he'd buried, the ones he'd tried to escape for so long, were now rushing in, forcing their way into his mind with a vengeance. The voice of the man—the one in the shadows—whispered from somewhere deep inside his mind, as though it had always been there.

"You can't escape me, Jason," the voice said, but it wasn't just a voice. It was a feeling, a presence that pressed against his skull, spreading through his body like ice, freezing him in place.

"No," Jason gasped, stumbling backward. His hands shot out in front of him, as if trying to ward off the invisible force that was suffocating him. "No, I don't remember. I don't want to remember."

Elle's eyes never left him as she stepped toward him, her movements slow and deliberate. Her presence seemed to pull the shadows closer, and Jason could feel them pressing against him, like a dark cloud enveloping him. "You have to remember, Jason. You have no choice."

"Stop," he pleaded, his voice breaking. His breath was ragged, his chest tight as he stumbled backward, tripping over his own feet. He hit the floor, hard, his palms scraping against the cold, unforgiving concrete. The pain was sharp, but it was nothing compared to the terror that had settled in his gut.

He could hear the whispers now, louder and clearer. The man's voice, the shadow in his memories. He could hear the words echoing through his mind, growing stronger with every second.

"You're mine, Jason. You always have been."

The walls around him seemed to close in, the mirrors now reflecting distorted versions of him. He could see himself—no, not himself—a different version of him, one with a twisted smile, his eyes empty, his soul hollow. A version that wasn't his. A version that shouldn't exist.

"Who are you?" Jason screamed, his voice raw with desperation. "What do you want from me?"

Elle stood over him now, her expression unreadable, almost as if she were watching him drown in his own fear. "You're not the man you think you are, Jason. Your life, everything you thought you knew... it's all a lie."

Jason could feel the room around him pulse with heat, the walls pressing in tighter, suffocating him. The shadow moved closer, a figure emerging from the darkness. It was him, or at least, a version of him. The man in the mirror—the one who wasn't him—stepped forward, his face twisted into a grin, his eyes burning with malice.

Jason gasped and scrambled to his feet, his legs shaking beneath him, but the figure—that figure—was already too close. The mirror version of himself reached out, his hand cold and unnatural, like the touch of death itself. Jason recoiled, but the shadow's fingers brushed against his cheek, sending a jolt of ice through his veins.

"Stop!" Jason cried, pushing the figure away, his heart pounding in his ears.

But the figure only laughed, the sound cruel and hollow, like it had no soul behind it. "You can't escape me, Jason. You never could."

Jason's head spun, his vision blurring with the realization of the impossible. The truth was slipping through his fingers like sand, but it was still there. He could feel it—deep inside him, buried beneath years of denial. He had to face it. He had to confront the man in the mirror, the man who had always been a part of him.

The man who had always been him.

"Get out of my head!" Jason screamed, his voice breaking, his hands pressed against his skull, as though trying to stop the flood of memories from overwhelming him.

But it was no use. The memories were flooding in faster now—too fast for him to process, too fast for him to fight.

Elle's voice broke through the chaos, calm and unwavering. "It's time to remember, Jason. Everything."

And in that moment, as the last threads of his sanity unraveled, Jason's world exploded into light.

The truth, horrifying and unrelenting, washed over him like a flood. He remembered. He remembered everything.

And it was worse than he could have ever imagined.

# 13

## The Unseen Hand

Jason's body was frozen, his mind a blur of distorted images and fragmented memories, each one more terrifying than the last. The room was spinning around him, the mirrors warping and twisting in unnatural shapes, reflecting faces that weren't his—faces of people he didn't know. The figure—the man who had stepped out of the mirror—was still there, standing in the shadows, watching him with an unsettling stillness.

He could feel the darkness creeping in, suffocating him with its cold grip. The air was heavy, pressing against his chest like a vice, making it impossible to breathe. His thoughts swirled together, disjointed, pieces of his past bleeding into the present, a tangled mess of confusion and fear.

"I didn't want to remember," Jason gasped, his voice cracking, barely a whisper against the oppressive silence. "I didn't want to know."

Elle's voice was soft, barely audible, but it felt like it was cutting through the fog in his mind, sharp and insistent. "You don't have a choice anymore, Jason. The truth is inside you, whether you want to face it or not."

The man in the shadows stepped closer, his figure solidifying as if the darkness itself was feeding him, growing him. Jason could feel the cold presence of the figure, pressing in on him, drawing closer and closer, until Jason was sure the space between them was nonexistent.

"You're mine," the figure's voice said, but it wasn't a voice. It was a sensation, a chill that curled into Jason's very soul, whispering in his ear. "Always have been."

Jason shook his head violently, trying to rid himself of the oppressive feeling that was consuming him. His heart pounded in his chest, a heavy, rhythmic thud that seemed to echo in his ears, drowning out everything else. He didn't want to hear it. He didn't want to accept what this thing was telling him.

But no matter how hard he tried, the truth refused to let him go. It was too powerful. It was too real.

Jason stepped back, his legs unsteady beneath him. His eyes darted around the room, searching for an escape, but the door they had entered through was now gone—replaced by the endless mirrors that reflected every possible angle of his torment. It was as though the room itself had become a living nightmare, bending and shifting, trapping him inside his own mind.

"Why are you doing this to me?" Jason screamed, his voice rising in panic. "Why now?"

Elle was still there, silent, her presence a constant weight on his back. Her figure seemed to blend into the darkness, almost as if she were part of it, her face a mask of impassivity.

"You think you have a choice, but you don't," she said softly, her tone cold and calculating. "You were always meant to face this. You were always meant to remember."

Jason's pulse quickened as the figure in the shadows took another step forward. The air around him seemed to grow colder, more suffocating. He couldn't move—he couldn't escape. His legs felt like they were made of lead, his body paralyzed by the weight of his own fear.

He could feel the man's presence now, right behind him, the cold breath of the figure against his skin. The whisper of its voice in his ear.

"You can't run anymore, Jason. You can't hide from what you are."

Jason turned quickly, his eyes wide with terror. But the figure was gone, vanished into thin air. He spun around in a circle, searching desperately for any sign of it, but it was as though the man had never existed.

Then, the room shifted.

The mirrors began to twist and distort, the reflections changing before his eyes. They no longer showed him and Elle—now they showed something else. Flashes of a life that wasn't his, flashes of places he'd never been, of people he didn't know.

A woman with blood on her hands. A child screaming for help. A man in the shadows, watching. Always watching.

"Make it stop!" Jason screamed, but the room only seemed to tighten around him. His vision blurred, his head spinning as more images flooded in—each one darker, each one more twisted.

In the reflection, he saw himself again. But this time, it wasn't just him. The man in the shadows was there too—standing behind him, his hand on his shoulder, as if claiming him, marking him. Jason's breath hitched. His mind screamed, but no sound came from his lips.

"No," he whispered, trembling. "No, this isn't me. This isn't real."

But as the figure in the reflection smiled, Jason's doubts began to crack. The smile was too familiar, too close. It mirrored his own, a twisted version of his own face. He felt the weight of the man's hand on his shoulder as if the figure had crossed over, stepping into the real world, its cold touch seeping into his bones.

"Stop!" Jason cried out, his voice hoarse with fear. "What do you want from me?"

The mirrors shattered, their glass falling in sharp, jagged pieces around him, but the images didn't stop. They continued to flash before his eyes, each one more horrifying than the last. The reflection of himself—no, the reflection of the man in the shadows—grew clearer with each passing second.

"You don't remember, do you?" the voice whispered again, its words curling around him like smoke. "You don't remember what you've done."

Jason's stomach lurched, the taste of bile rising in his throat. The floor beneath him seemed to shift, warping like the mirrors, and he stumbled, falling to his knees, clutching his head in his hands. The weight of the memories pressing down on him felt unbearable, as though the entire world was closing in, suffocating him.

"You—" Jason gasped. "You did this to me."

Elle finally stepped forward, her voice still as cold as ice. "No, Jason. You did this to yourself. You've always known. You've just been too afraid to see it."

Jason's mind reeled. He could barely breathe. The shadows in the room seemed to multiply, to spread like a sickness, suffocating him from all sides. The whispers were louder now, overwhelming him, telling him things he wasn't ready to hear. His mind was a battlefield, every thought a battle, every word a wound.

"No," he whispered again, but this time, there was no defiance in his voice. Only a deep, resounding terror.

The man in the shadows was everywhere now. In the mirrors. In his head. Everywhere.

"You think you're free," the voice continued, "but you're not. You were never free."

Jason's body trembled, the words sinking into his bones, paralyzing him with their weight. He couldn't move. He couldn't breathe.

His mind swirled with images. The shadowy figure. The bloodied woman. The child screaming for help. The darkness that had followed him, that had always followed him.

"Help," Jason gasped, the word escaping his lips like a prayer. "Someone, help me."

But there was no help. There was no escape.

As the darkness closed in, and the memories he had tried so desperately to forget flooded over him, Jason realized the truth.

The truth was that he had never been in control. The unseen hand that had guided him—watched him—had always been there, and now, it was too late.

The truth was coming for him.

And it wasn't going to let him go.

# 14

## Beneath the Surface

Jason's chest heaved with every breath, his heart a frantic drumbeat in his chest. His hands were slick with sweat, fingers trembling as they gripped the cold, cracked tile floor beneath him. The room around him seemed to warp, the shadows flickering and growing taller, more menacing, until they consumed the edges of the walls, drowning him in darkness. The air tasted bitter, metallic, like iron, and he could feel the weight of it pushing down on him, suffocating him.

It's not real. It can't be real. The thought spiraled in his mind, but the images, the voices, wouldn't let him go. They were everywhere. In his head. In his blood. In his bones. He couldn't escape them.

A faint ringing sound echoed in his ears, growing louder and louder with every passing second. He squeezed his eyes shut, trying to block it out, but the sound only intensified, reverberating through his skull.

"Jason."

Elle's voice came from the shadows, soft and distant, but it cut through the cacophony in his head like a knife. Jason's heart skipped a beat, his body stiffening at the sound. He opened his eyes, and there she was, standing in the doorway, her silhouette outlined by the faint glow of the flickering light above her. Her expression was unreadable, her eyes dark pools of mystery.

"You shouldn't have come back," Jason muttered under his breath, his voice cracking.

Elle stepped forward, her movements slow, deliberate. Her gaze never wavered, as though she were seeing through him, beyond the mask of fear and confusion that he had carefully constructed.

"You can't run from what's inside you, Jason," Elle said softly, her voice like velvet, smooth and dangerous. "It's always been there, waiting for you to wake up."

Jason backed away, his hands pressed flat against the floor as he scrambled to his feet. His thoughts were a tangled mess, his head pounding with every heartbeat, the sound of his own pulse ringing in his ears. He felt trapped—trapped in his own mind, in this room, in this life that wasn't his. The walls seemed to close in around him, pressing on him from all sides, and every shadow, every flicker of light, felt like it was alive, watching him, waiting for him to make a move.

"I don't know what you're talking about," he rasped, his voice trembling. "I don't—I don't remember."

Elle's eyes narrowed, her lips curling into a faint smile. "Oh, but you do, Jason. You do. Deep down, you know exactly what's happening here."

Jason could feel the ground beneath him shift, as though the very earth were twisting and turning beneath his feet. The room began to pulse, the shadows stretching and contracting like a living thing. A cold wind blew through the cracked windows, howling like a mournful cry, and the floor beneath him seemed to hum with a low, ominous vibration.

The ringing in his ears grew louder, piercing, until it was deafening. It was a sound that didn't belong to the world he knew, a sound that felt as though it were coming from somewhere far beneath the surface—somewhere he couldn't reach. Somewhere that no one could.

Jason's breath caught in his throat, and he turned his head, his eyes darting toward the far corner of the room. At first, he thought he had imagined it, but then, there it was again—the movement in the shadows, the flicker of something—or someone—just out of sight.

"No," he whispered, taking a cautious step back. "No, not again."

But it wasn't a hallucination. The figure stepped forward, out of the darkness, its shape becoming clearer as it emerged from the shadows. It was a man—tall, his features sharp and cold, his eyes glinting with an unsettling intelligence. Jason felt his stomach drop. The man was familiar, but not in a way he could place. The recognition was there, lurking just beneath the surface, like a dark secret he'd buried long ago.

"Who are you?" Jason demanded, his voice shaky, his body tense with fear.

The man didn't speak. Instead, he stepped forward, and Jason's heart skipped a beat. It was as though the very air around him had thickened, becoming harder to breathe. Every step the man took seemed to pull Jason deeper into the nightmare, into the suffocating, cold grip of something he couldn't escape.

Elle's voice came again, quiet, almost too soft to hear. "You've been running from him for years, Jason. But he's never left."

The man stopped just a few feet away from Jason, his eyes fixed on him with an intensity that made Jason's skin crawl. He reached out, his hand hovering just inches from Jason's face, and Jason flinched, stepping back. The air felt electric, charged with a danger that made his hair stand on end.

"You're still here," Jason said, his voice barely a whisper. "You never left."

The man's lips curled into a slow, cruel smile. "You've always known I'd be here, Jason. You just didn't want to see it."

Jason's knees buckled, and he stumbled backward, falling to the floor. His hands trembled, reaching for something, anything to hold onto. But there was nothing. The world was slipping away from him, spinning out of control. He couldn't escape the feeling that something was clawing at him, something deep inside, something he didn't want to confront.

And then, the whisper came.

It wasn't from the man. It wasn't from Elle. It wasn't even from the air around him.

It was in his mind.

"You're mine," the voice said, a low, guttural sound that sent a shiver down his spine. "You always have been."

Jason's breath caught in his throat. The words felt like a dark promise, a threat from something that had been lurking in the shadows, waiting for the right moment to claim him. The room seemed to tilt, the walls closing in, the ground shifting beneath him.

"I—" Jason began, but the words died on his lips. He couldn't form them. He couldn't understand the overwhelming pressure in his mind, the crushing weight of something he couldn't grasp. His hands reached for his head, clutching at his hair, his thoughts spiraling out of control.

The man, still standing there, watching with cold eyes, stepped forward once again. This time, his hand reached down, brushing against Jason's arm, his fingers cold and unfeeling.

Jason recoiled, his skin prickling with a deep, gnawing fear. He tried to move, tried to get away, but it was like he was trapped in place, frozen in time, unable to escape the force that was pulling him under.

"No!" Jason cried out, his voice raw with desperation. "No more! I can't—I can't take it anymore!"

But the man's hand was on his shoulder now, a heavy, unrelenting pressure. Jason could feel the cold creeping into his skin, into his soul. He could feel the weight of the past, the dark truths he had buried, all rising to the surface.

"You can't escape the past, Jason," the man said, his voice smooth, almost gentle. "It's already inside you. And now... you will remember everything."

Jason's pulse raced, his vision blurring, and in that moment, the room seemed to shatter. The shadows closed in, and the figure's hand tightened on his shoulder, dragging him down into the darkness.

The surface was broken. The truth, the memories, everything Jason had been running from, was finally coming to the surface.

And there was no escaping it.

Not now.

Not ever.

# 15

## Into the Abyss

Jason awoke with a jolt, his body jerking upright as if he had been dragged from the depths of a nightmare. The breath in his lungs felt thick, as if something was choking him from the inside, but his hands moved quickly to his throat—nothing was there. No hands. No chains.

Just silence.

But the silence felt wrong. It was the kind of silence that presses down on you, heavy and suffocating. He could feel it crawling under his skin, moving like an unseen shadow through the marrow of his bones. His heart thundered against his ribcage, each beat reverberating like a drum, loud enough to drown out the sound of his own thoughts. The air was thick with the remnants of something... something dark that he couldn't place, couldn't understand.

Where was he?

He looked around. The walls of the room were unfamiliar—bleak and cold, stone instead of the crumbling wood he'd left behind. The room itself was dim, lit by a single flickering bulb that hung like a lost star. His surroundings were barren, save for a small table in the corner, covered in dust, its surface reflecting the pale glow of the light above. But there was something else, too, something that made his stomach churn, something watching him.

He could feel it in the pit of his stomach—a gnawing sensation, like the echo of something waiting to emerge.

Jason stood up, his legs unsteady beneath him, and immediately, he felt the pull of the shadows again. A shift in the air, a twinge of discomfort that made his spine straighten. He glanced at the door—it was slightly ajar, the faintest sliver of darkness beyond it. His instincts screamed at him to stay where he was, to lock the door, to hide from whatever was coming.

But Jason wasn't that person anymore. He wasn't going to let the shadows dictate his life anymore. He wasn't going to let the darkness win. At least... that's what he told himself.

He moved toward the door slowly, as if the very act of stepping into the hallway beyond could set off a chain of events he wasn't ready for. The floorboards creaked beneath him with each step, the sound sharp and disturbing in the stillness.

There's something here. Something I can't see. Something I don't understand.

The thought clawed at his mind, but he pushed it aside. He had to keep moving. He had to get out of this place—he had to get out before it was too late.

He reached the door and nudged it open with the tip of his foot, the hinge squeaking in protest. The hallway beyond was long and narrow, the walls lined with faded portraits whose eyes seemed to follow him, shifting unnervingly with each step he took. The air smelled damp, like the bowels of a forgotten building, thick and musty, with the faintest hint of decay.

Jason hesitated, his heart racing again. Every instinct he had screamed at him to turn back, to retreat into the room and lock the door again. But he couldn't do it. Not now.

He stepped out into the hallway, and the door clicked softly shut behind him.

At first, everything seemed eerily still, the silence pressing in from all sides. But then it came—softly at first—a faint whisper in the air, like the rustling of pages or the distant hum of a voice just on the edge of hearing.

Jason froze.

It was the voice again. The voice that had been haunting him for days, perhaps weeks—he couldn't tell anymore. But it wasn't Elle's voice, and it wasn't the voice of the man in the shadows. It was... something else. Something older. Something buried.

The whisper came again, clearer this time. "Jason..."

He spun around, looking for the source of the voice, his heart racing with a frantic urgency. But there was nothing. No one. The hallway was empty, the portraits still staring at him with their hollow eyes, their painted faces etched with an expression of... knowing.

"Who's there?" Jason called out, his voice shaking with the weight of the fear pressing against his chest. But there was no response—just the echo of his own words, reverberating down the long hallway.

Jason's breath came in ragged gasps as he began to walk, his feet moving quicker now, his pace faster, almost desperate. The hallway seemed to stretch ahead of him endlessly, no doors, no windows, just walls and shadows that played tricks on his eyes. With every step he took, he felt as though the darkness were closing in, that something—someone—was following him. Watching him.

And then, ahead of him, at the far end of the hall, something moved.

A figure.

It was barely a shadow, a glimpse of movement that vanished the moment his eyes locked onto it. Jason froze. His body went cold as ice. His pulse thundered in his ears.

No. No, no, no...

The voice came again, this time clearer, more insistent.

"Jason, you can't escape."

He wanted to turn and run. He wanted to find some place to hide, to shut himself away from whatever was chasing him, whatever had followed him into this place. But his feet refused to move. He was paralyzed, rooted to the spot, staring into the darkness ahead of him, waiting for whatever was coming next.

The figure appeared again, this time more solid, a faint outline against the shadows. And then, it stepped into the light.

It was a woman.

Elle.

But not Elle in the way he remembered her. This version of her was... different. Her face was drawn and pale, her eyes wide and unnaturally dark. She was smiling, but there was no warmth in it—only an emptiness that made Jason's blood run cold.

"Elle?" Jason whispered, his voice barely audible.

But she didn't respond. She only stood there, watching him with those cold, unblinking eyes, as if she were waiting for him to do something. Waiting for him to remember.

And then, just as suddenly as she appeared, she vanished—disappearing back into the shadows from where she came.

Jason's breath caught in his throat. He didn't know what he had just seen. Didn't know what it meant. But it wasn't real. It couldn't be real.

But then... something tugged at the back of his mind. A memory. A thought. A name.

"Elle...?" Jason called again, this time louder, his voice shaking with fear. But there was no answer.

The silence returned.

But Jason knew it wasn't the silence he had come to understand. This silence was different. It was the kind of silence that came before the storm, the kind that filled the air with an unbearable tension.

And then, from the end of the hallway, the door that had been left ajar slammed shut.

The sound reverberated through the building, a sharp crack that felt like the break of something fragile. Jason turned toward the door, his feet moving faster now, panic rising like a fire in his chest. His eyes were wide, his breath quick and shallow, and the shadows seemed to lengthen around him, creeping closer, coiling at his heels.

But as he reached for the door, something stopped him.

A hand.

A cold, skeletal hand gripped his wrist, freezing him in place. Jason spun around, his pulse spiking, only to find... nothing. No one there.

Except for the shadows, growing darker and thicker, crawling in from all sides, swallowing the light.

The door behind him groaned, creaking like it was alive, and Jason's body tensed, his mind screaming at him to run.

But it was already too late.

The abyss was waiting for him.

And he was already falling into it.

# 16

# The Silent Watcher

Jason's breath was shallow, his chest tight with a fear he could not escape. His hand trembled as he reached for the doorknob, the cold metal seeping through his skin like ice. The shadows behind him grew darker, more oppressive, pressing against the walls, the floor, the ceiling, as if the very building were breathing with a life of its own. The hairs on the back of his neck stood on end, each second that passed dragging him deeper into a nightmare that no longer felt like a dream.

He wrenched open the door, but it didn't matter. The hallway beyond was the same as it had been—long, narrow, and endless, stretching far into darkness, as if it were designed to trap him, to pull him into a void where time ceased to exist.

And yet, something was different this time.

Jason's pulse quickened. His heart hammered in his chest as he stepped into the hallway, cautiously scanning his surroundings. The air was thick with the smell of something ancient—dust and mildew, yes, but underneath it, something heavier. Something wrong. The silence that enveloped him was no longer comforting; it was suffocating, thick with a presence that felt like it was lurking just behind his shoulder, waiting for him to turn around.

And then he heard it—a soft, barely audible sound, like the scuffing of footsteps against the floor. The sound was unmistakable, too close to be ignored, but when he turned, the hallway was empty. His breath caught, his legs froze in place.

No one.

But then—there it was again.

A shadow. A flicker of movement at the edge of his vision. Jason's head snapped toward it, but the hallway was still, the walls empty. The sound had stopped. For a moment, there was nothing but the thrum of his own heartbeat pounding in his ears. But it didn't take long for the dread to set in again, curling around his chest like an iron fist.

Something was watching him. Something that wasn't supposed to be there.

He started walking, trying to convince himself that it was all in his head, that the shadows were simply shadows, and the noise was nothing more than the house settling. But the further he went, the more he couldn't shake the feeling that the darkness was alive, breathing with him, watching with him.

Jason's eyes darted from one end of the hallway to the other. The flickering lights above him buzzed softly, casting uneven shadows across the walls. The portraits on the walls—once ordinary pieces of forgotten art—now seemed to take on a more sinister quality. Their faces, blurred and indistinct, shifted when he wasn't looking directly at them, as if they were alive. Their eyes followed him with a quiet, knowing gaze, and Jason's stomach twisted with each passing second.

There was no denying it anymore. He wasn't alone.

And whoever—or whatever—was here, was waiting for him.

His pulse surged as the footsteps sounded again, unmistakably closer this time, the scuff of shoes against wood growing louder, more distinct, echoing through the hallway. He turned sharply, his heart racing. The door at the far end of the corridor stood ajar. It hadn't been that way before. He knew it.

Who's there? Jason thought, his voice lodged in his throat. He couldn't speak the words aloud. He couldn't admit what his mind was telling him. That the fear wasn't just a product of his imagination. That it was real.

The door opened wider.

Jason stepped forward, his legs shaking with each step. The sound of his breathing felt deafening, but there was no other noise. No more footsteps, no more whispering. Just the same silence that pressed against his skull, as if the walls themselves were trying to crush him.

With each step he took toward the door, the feeling of dread thickened, growing until it was almost suffocating. When his fingers brushed against the doorframe, a coldness surged through him, spreading up his arm like a dark current. His skin prickled, and his breath caught in his throat.

The door swung open completely with a low, mournful creak, revealing a room that was nothing like he had expected.

It was a study—dark, dimly lit by a single, flickering candle on a desk piled high with papers. Books lined the shelves, but none of the titles were visible. They seemed to shift, warping into shapes that Jason couldn't quite decipher. The air in the room felt charged, heavy with a presence that made the hairs on the back of his neck stand on end.

And then he saw it.

At the far side of the room, standing in the corner, was a figure. Tall, thin, cloaked in black. The figure didn't move, didn't breathe. It simply stood there, facing the wall as though waiting for something.

Jason's blood ran cold. His legs felt like lead, the weight of fear pushing him down into the floor, preventing him from moving. He knew, deep down, that this was no ordinary figure. This wasn't a man. It wasn't even a living thing. It was something else. Something that should not be here, but was.

And then, it turned.

The movement was slow, deliberate. The figure's head tilted at an unnatural angle, as though it were studying him, evaluating him like prey. Its eyes—if they could even be called eyes—were two dark pits, voids that seemed to suck in the light around them. They were empty. Hungry. Unforgiving.

Jason's breath hitched as the figure stepped forward, its long limbs moving in a way that seemed both fluid and unnatural, like a marionette on strings.

A voice—soft, dry, and rasping—came from the depths of its throat.

"You've been running for so long, Jason."

Jason's heart stopped.

He didn't recognize the voice, but somehow, it felt like it belonged to him. It felt like a voice that had been inside him all along, waiting for the right moment to make itself known.

"You don't have to run anymore," the figure continued, its voice growing louder, more insistent. "The game is over."

Jason shook his head, trying to force the words from his mouth, trying to make them coherent. "What... what are you? What do you want from me?"

The figure's smile was slow, stretching unnaturally wide, revealing jagged, needle-like teeth that gleamed in the dim candlelight. "We've always been here, Jason. You've always known it, deep down. You just chose not to see."

The darkness around Jason seemed to pulse with the figure's words, expanding, closing in. It was as if the room itself was bending to its will, warping around him. He could hear the walls groaning, the ceiling cracking, the very air shuddering as if it were alive. The whispers began again, louder this time, overlapping, as though they were coming from everywhere, all at once.

Jason stepped back, his mind racing, but his body refused to move. The figure's voice seemed to wrap itself around him like a straitjacket.

"You can't escape what's inside of you, Jason," the figure hissed, stepping closer, its hands reaching toward him with fingers that were far too long. "The darkness is yours. And it always will be."

Jason's chest constricted with a panic that stole his breath. His pulse thrummed painfully in his temples, his thoughts scattered, his body frozen in place by an overwhelming force that he couldn't understand. His knees buckled, and he collapsed to the floor.

But the figure didn't stop.

It stepped forward, its shadow overtaking Jason's own. And as it reached out to touch him, everything went black.

For a brief, terrifying moment, there was nothing.

Then, a single whisper cut through the silence.

"You've always been mine."

# 17

## Beneath the Surface

Jason's eyes snapped open, but the world around him was still a blur, a vortex of shadows and dim light that twisted his perception. He could feel the weight of the darkness pressing in, suffocating him, yet his body was still frozen, paralyzed by the sheer force of what had just happened. The cold stone beneath him felt like it was seeping into his bones, numbing him from the inside out, and he could barely breathe as if the very air had turned to something thick and suffocating, a poisonous fog that clouded his senses.

Where am I?

The thought barely made it through his mind, but the answer was immediate and obvious: nowhere. No way out. The walls seemed to close in on him, their jagged edges creeping like tendrils, weaving through his thoughts and obscuring his vision. He had no sense of time—no sense of anything, really. All he could hear was the pounding of his heart, louder and louder with each passing moment, as if his body were screaming for release, for escape.

His limbs refused to obey him. The panic surged again—harder, fiercer. The shadow, that... thing, it was still here, somewhere. It was watching him. It had always been watching him. And Jason knew that if he didn't move, if he didn't get out of whatever hellish trap this was, he would become part of it. Part of them.

He clenched his teeth, trying to push the wave of terror aside. He had to think. He had to do something. But as he forced himself to move, his body screamed in protest, as if it was being held in place by invisible chains. The room around him was eerily still, too still, and yet he could feel the weight of unseen eyes on him, cold and unblinking.

Jason forced his fingers to twitch. A slow movement, just enough to reassure himself that his body was still capable of action. A tiny victory. His pulse quickened in response to the smallest bit of control he had regained, but it was fleeting. A tremor ran down his spine, and he couldn't ignore it.

The coldness. It was still here.

Suddenly, the silence shattered—a soft, almost imperceptible scrape, followed by a low, guttural sound, like the scrape of something against stone. Jason's heart skipped a beat. The noise was unmistakable, closer now. He wasn't alone. Not in the way he had been thinking. No, this was something else—something far worse.

The sound grew louder, closer. Someone—or something—was moving toward him, its steps slow, deliberate. There was no mistaking the presence now; the air seemed to bend around the shape, twisting and warping. Jason's breath hitched, his body trembling uncontrollably as he struggled to sit up. He needed to run, to escape, but the movement was slow, as if something was holding him back, something invisible that weighed on his chest.

His head snapped toward the noise, his body frozen in terror as he saw the shadow in the corner of the room. It was still indistinct, shapeless, but it was growing clearer—closer. A whisper—just a faint breath against his ear—sent ice running through his veins.

"You're not getting away that easily."

Jason's heart plummeted. It was the same voice. That cold, rasping tone that had haunted him for what felt like an eternity. But it wasn't just the voice—it was the thing attached to it. The creature, the shadow that followed him, fed on him, used him.

It had been with him all along.

A hand—pale, almost translucent—reached from the darkness, fingers stretching toward him like gnarled branches. Jason's body screamed for him to move, but all he could do was stare, transfixed by the hand, watching as it hovered inches from his face.

He gasped, pulling back, and finally, his body responded,

propelling him backward, away from the thing that had haunted him in every shadow. But even as he scrambled to stand, to run, his feet slipped. The floor beneath him was slick, like oil, or something worse, and his arms flailed to catch himself, but he crashed hard against the cold stone. His chest tightened in pain, but the worse pain—the real agony—was the feeling that he was still trapped. Trapped in this nightmare.

The shadow was now at the edge of his vision, its dark, void-like figure standing motionless, waiting. But Jason couldn't stop his heart from racing faster. The weight of the thing's presence pressed on him like a physical force, like a vise around his ribcage. It wasn't just a presence. It was a trap. He was stuck, suffocating under its grasp, and every instinct in him told him that it wasn't the darkness he should fear.

It was what was in it.

The figure in the corner moved again, and this time, Jason saw it clearly. It was a face—pale, gaunt, eyes sunken deep into a hollow skull. The lips peeled back in an unnatural smile, revealing rows of jagged teeth, sharp and yellowed. It was grinning at him, its eyes flashing with something dark, something familiar, something Jason had hoped he could forget.

"Elle?" Jason whispered, his voice trembling.

But it wasn't her. Not really. No, this was a distortion, an abomination. It was everything that Elle had become after the darkness had claimed her. It was a twisted version of her, a reflection of something that had once been beautiful, now reduced to an empty shell.

Her—its—voice came again, softer, but louder in Jason's mind.

"You were never meant to escape, Jason. You've always belonged here, beneath the surface. We've always been waiting."

Jason's heart pounded harder. The fear that rose in him was suffocating, but still, he couldn't look away. This thing—it knew him. It understood him in a way no one else did. The weight of it—of her—was so overwhelming that he couldn't tell if his mind was breaking, or if the world around him was. Was this real? Was anything real?

"You've been running from the truth." The thing's smile deepened, stretching impossibly wide, too wide to be natural. "But you can't hide from it anymore."

The air around Jason grew thicker, more oppressive, as the thing moved closer. It was right beside him now, its eyes glowing faintly in the darkness. He could hear its breath, shallow and rasping, mingling with his own. And in that moment, Jason understood.

The fear. The darkness. The endless running.

It was all his. It had always been a part of him. And no matter where he went, no matter how far he tried to run, it would never let him go.

Because the darkness was inside him.

And that was the thing he could never escape.

With the realization crashing down on him like a tidal wave, Jason collapsed back onto the cold stone, his chest tight, his breath ragged. The walls closed in, the shadows consuming him completely.

He was trapped. But not by the building. Not by the thing in the corner.

He was trapped by himself.

And there was no way out.

The last thing he heard before the world fell into complete darkness was the soft whisper of the thing's voice, curling into his mind like a poisoned lullaby.

"Welcome home, Jason."

And then, there was nothing.

# 18

## The Echo of Lies

Jason awoke with a jolt, his body jerking upright from the cold stone floor. The darkness still clung to him, thick and suffocating, wrapping around him like a shroud. His breath came in short gasps, sharp and ragged, but there was no comfort in the inhalation. The air was thick with the scent of decay, of something old and forgotten, and his skin felt clammy, cold as if he had been lying there for hours—or days.

He didn't know where he was anymore.

The last thing he remembered was the shadow, the twisted reflection of Elle, its voice echoing in his ears, telling him the truth. Or was it? His mind struggled to hold onto fragments of reality, but everything was slipping away, like sand through his fingers.

"Welcome home, Jason." The words whispered through his thoughts, an echo that reverberated with terrifying clarity. The voice that belonged to her—or something that used to be her—

still echoed in his mind, rattling his nerves, tearing apart the last remnants of his sanity. Had he really been trapped all along? Had this dark force always been a part of him?

He pushed the thought away with a shudder. He couldn't think about that right now. He needed to focus. He needed to escape.

Jason staggered to his feet, the world spinning around him. The room was empty—no shadows lurking in the corners, no figure watching from the darkness. Just the oppressive quiet, the walls looming like giants, closing in around him with every step he took. But the silence itself felt wrong. The room was empty, but the space seemed... alive—alive with secrets, alive with lies.

He reached out for the nearest wall, his fingers brushing against the cold, rough surface. It felt like a lifeline, something to ground him in the reality he so desperately needed to hold onto. But as his hand pressed against it, a wave of unease washed over him.

Something was different.

The air had shifted. Jason's heart began to pound harder in his chest. He could feel the subtle vibrations beneath his fingertips, the faint hum of the walls, almost like they were breathing with him, moving with him. The world was alive, but it wasn't right.

Without warning, the floor beneath him trembled—just a slight shift, a quiver, as though the very foundation of the building was buckling under the weight of an unseen force. Jason stumbled backward, his eyes darting around the room, scanning every corner for any sign of movement. But there was nothing. No figure, no shadow. Just that oppressive silence, that suffocating presence that he could never quite escape.

A low, groaning sound echoed through the walls, followed by a sharp cracking noise. Jason's head whipped toward the source of the sound. The door. The heavy wooden door at the far side of the room was shifting, creaking on its hinges, as though something was trying to force its way through.

He froze, the blood draining from his face.

Something was coming.

His mind raced, his body instinctively moving toward the door, even though every fiber of his being screamed to run in the opposite direction. But it was too late. The door was already beginning to open, slowly, deliberately, as if whatever was behind it was savoring the moment.

Jason's heart thudded in his chest, and his body locked in place. The door opened a crack, then another, until the gap was wide enough for him to see a sliver of what lay beyond: a hallway, bathed in shadows, stretching out into the unknown. But it wasn't just the hallway that made Jason's blood run cold—it was the sound, the unmistakable sound of breathing, low and labored, coming from the other side.

The creature.

His hand trembled as it reached for the door handle, the cold metal sending a shiver up his arm. He couldn't go through there—not again. Not after everything he had just faced. But he couldn't stay here either. He had no choice.

With one last, desperate glance at the room behind him, Jason pulled the door open and stepped into the hallway.

Immediately, the temperature seemed to drop, the air growing colder with every breath. His feet moved instinctively, taking slow, careful steps as he made his way down the darkened corridor. The flickering lights above him buzzed erratically, casting fleeting shadows that seemed to move on their own. Every footstep felt like it echoed in the vast emptiness of the space.

But there was no silence.

The whispers had started again.

At first, they were distant—just faint murmurs, too soft to understand. But as he walked deeper into the hallway, they grew louder, clearer, until they were all he could hear. Their voices crawled beneath his skin, filling his mind with words he couldn't understand but could feel. Each syllable seemed to twist his thoughts, turning them against him, until he wasn't sure what was real anymore.

He stopped abruptly, his breath caught in his throat. He wasn't alone.

A figure stood at the far end of the hallway.

It was just a silhouette at first, a shadow against the flickering light, but as Jason's eyes focused, the figure became clearer. A woman. Tall, slender, her long hair flowing around her like a cloak. She wore a dress, but there was something wrong with it—its color, its texture—it shimmered unnaturally, as though it were made of something else entirely, something alive. Her face was obscured by shadows, but Jason could feel her presence—strong, overpowering, pressing down on him, suffocating him.

The whispers were now louder, more urgent, as if they were coming from her, or from the very walls around him.

"Elle?" Jason whispered, his voice cracking with fear.

But the woman didn't answer.

She didn't move either. She just stood there, waiting.

His heart pounded in his chest, the blood rushing in his ears. Something about her... It was familiar. Too familiar. It was the way she stood—her posture, the way the shadows clung to her like a second skin. It was almost like... like he had seen her before.

No. No, it wasn't her.

This wasn't Elle.

This was something else. Something far worse.

A sound, low and guttural, broke the silence. It was a laugh—a dry, wheezing laugh that sent a chill running down Jason's spine. The figure in front of him stepped forward, her eyes gleaming with a sickening light.

And that's when Jason saw it—saw her face.

It wasn't Elle. It was a twisted mockery of her, a reflection of everything Jason had loved, now corrupted, distorted beyond recognition. Her face was pale, gaunt, her eyes wide and black as night, devoid of any warmth, any humanity. Her lips curled into a smile that was both cruel and familiar.

"You should never have come back, Jason." Her voice rasped, harsh and grating, like nails on a chalkboard.

Jason's breath hitched. "What... what are you?"

"I'm the truth you've been running from." She took another step toward him, her smile widening. "You can't escape me. You can't escape yourself."

Jason stumbled backward, his mind racing. He couldn't breathe, couldn't think—all of it was closing in on him. The walls, the whispers, the thing before him—it was all one thing. He wasn't running from a creature, or from a ghost, or from Elle. He was running from himself.

And no matter where he went, no matter what he did, it would always find him.

The woman stepped forward again, her movements unnaturally smooth, her eyes never leaving his.

"You've been lying to yourself for so long, Jason. But now, the truth will come for you."

Jason spun around, panic surging in his veins. There was no escape. Not from her. Not from the truth. Not from the lies that had haunted him for so long. The hallway stretched out in front of him, endless and dark, with no end in sight.

But the truth, as it always does, was catching up.

And this time, there was nowhere to run.

As the woman's hand reached out to touch him, the walls closed in around him, and everything went black.

And in that moment, Jason understood.

He had never left.

He had always been here.

# 19

## The Weight of Shadows

Jason's eyes snapped open, but the world before him was as disorienting as it had been when he'd first lost consciousness. The air felt thick, charged with something he couldn't name. His chest tightened, and panic surged through him, like a rising tide pulling him under. The shadows that had haunted him were still there, even though his surroundings were unfamiliar. He couldn't shake the feeling that they were waiting—waiting for him to remember, to understand something that had eluded him for far too long.

The first thing Jason noticed was the cold. The air bit at his skin, a sharp, biting chill that seemed to wrap around his bones, sinking deep into his marrow. His breath came in shallow bursts, visible in the dim light of the room. The walls were made of stone, rough and uneven, like the inside of a forgotten prison cell, and the floor was covered in layers of dust, untouched by any sign of life. The smell was damp, musty—decay hung in the air, thick and oppressive.

He tried to move, but his body refused to obey him. The feeling of paralysis, of being trapped, returned with a vengeance, pinning him to the ground like a weight he couldn't lift. His fingers twitched, his muscles screamed, but his limbs felt heavy, as if they were weighed down by chains, invisible but crushing.

No. Not again.

He forced himself to breathe, slow and steady, as he focused on the sensations that surrounded him. There was a soft, constant hum in the air—like a buzzing, a vibration deep in his chest, something that felt both foreign and familiar. It was as if the very room itself was alive, pulsing with an energy that he couldn't comprehend. It was then that he realized: he wasn't alone.

A shadow, darker than the rest, shifted against the far wall, its form indistinct but moving. Jason's heart skipped a beat. He strained his eyes, trying to focus, but the darkness played tricks on him, shifting and warping before his very gaze.

Something is here. Something is waiting.

He tried to speak, but his voice was lodged in his throat, caught somewhere between panic and disbelief. His pulse thundered in his ears, the blood rushing like a river that was about to burst its banks. He could feel the presence creeping closer, could almost sense the weight of it, like a shadow passing over him.

"Jason." The voice came again, that same low, rasping whisper that sent a chill through his very core.

It was her.

Elle.

But it wasn't.

Jason's heart stuttered, and he blinked rapidly, trying to clear his mind. He was trapped in a labyrinth of darkness and confusion, unable to separate the truth from the lie. He couldn't tell if this was another hallucination, another manifestation of the twisted nightmares that had plagued him for what seemed like an eternity—or if this was real.

It doesn't matter, he realized. It doesn't matter whether it's real or not. This—whatever this is—is real.

He forced his body to move, his muscles aching with the effort. It was as though the weight of the room, of the shadows, was pressing down on him, trying to crush him into submission. But he couldn't give in. Not now. Not when he was this close. He just needed to reach the door, to find the exit. To get out of here.

But as he crawled toward the far side of the room, the shadows seemed to lengthen, stretching across the floor like tendrils, curling and wrapping around his legs, pulling him back. Jason gritted his teeth against the rising panic, but his chest tightened with every move he made. The walls seemed to pulse, the air thickening, suffocating him.

"You can't escape me," the voice whispered, closer now. "Not again."

Jason's blood ran cold. He froze, his hand outstretched toward the door. It was just within reach. But the words were like a curse, wrapping around him like chains, heavy and unrelenting.

Elle…

No, it wasn't Elle. This was not her.

A shape appeared in the doorway, blocking the faint light that filtered in from beyond. It was a figure—a tall, indistinct shape, cloaked in darkness. But even in the dim light, Jason could feel the presence of it, as if the very room recoiled from the creature standing in the doorway. He couldn't make out its features, but the cold radiating from it felt like a wave crashing over him, sinking deep into his skin.

He was too slow.

The figure moved with unnatural speed, closing the gap between them in an instant. Jason's breath hitched as he scrambled backward, but his body still felt sluggish, heavy, unwilling to obey. A cold hand—no, not a hand—a claw, long and jagged, reached out to him, curling around his wrist with a force that made him gasp.

And in that moment, the world seemed to tilt.

Jason's vision blurred, the edges of his sight darkening as though the very fabric of reality was pulling away. The room spun around him, and he could hear the faint echo of whispers—those voices again, speaking in fragments, in riddles that made no sense.

"You've been here before," the voice murmured. "And you'll be here again."

Jason's heart pounded in his chest, a wild, desperate rhythm, but his body felt numb, caught between the agony of fear and the heavy weight of something else—something far worse than fear itself. He could feel the pressure of the shadow's grip, its claws digging into his skin, sending a jolt of icy terror through his veins.

He was being pulled toward it, toward the darkness that seemed to engulf everything. And as the figure's face came into view, Jason's breath caught in his throat.

It wasn't just Elle. It was them. All of them. All the shadows that had haunted him, the figures that had followed him through every moment of his life, twisted versions of himself, of Elle, of everything he had ever feared. They were here. In the room with him.

And now they were closing in.

Jason's vision was fading, but he could still hear the voice, still feel the pressure of the shadow surrounding him. He was slipping away, losing himself in the darkness, but something deep inside him—something primal—fought against it.

I won't die here, Jason thought fiercely, his mind sparking with defiance. I won't let it take me.

His hands scrambled for something—anything—to hold on to. His fingers brushed against the cold stone of the floor, finding a jagged edge, a crack in the surface. His breath came in shallow, frantic bursts as he pulled himself forward, inch by inch, trying to break free from the grasp of the shadow.

The whispering voices grew louder, pressing in on him, drowning out everything else. He could hear them now—each word clear, each syllable like a weight that crushed him further.

"You belong to the darkness."

But Jason refused to listen. He was still here. He was still alive. And that meant there was still hope.

With a sudden, violent surge of strength, Jason pushed himself upright, his body screaming in protest, but he didn't care. His vision swam, but he focused on the light—the faint light at the far end of the room. There was no time to think. No time for fear. Only one thing mattered now.

He ran.

Each step felt like an eternity, his heart pounding in his chest, his feet slipping on the slick, uneven floor. The shadows seemed to shift and pulse with him, chasing him, but he couldn't stop. Not now.

He reached the door.

But as his hand wrapped around the handle, he heard it again.

The whisper.

"You will never escape."

And then, the world went dark.

But Jason didn't stop. Not this time.

He had to keep going.

Even if the darkness was already inside him.

# 20

## The Cage of Truth

Jason's feet hit the cold stone floor with a dull thud as he stumbled backward, his heart racing. The darkness pressed against him, a heavy weight that seemed to invade his every breath, suffocating him. He tried to focus, to steady his mind, but the walls around him were closing in with a quiet, unrelenting menace. It was as if the entire space was alive, breathing with him, watching him.

The door slammed shut behind him with a deafening crash, the sound echoing through the room like the roar of a thunderclap. He turned in a blind panic, his pulse pounding in his ears, but there was nothing but shadow and stone—no way out. No escape.

This isn't real. This can't be real. Jason's mind screamed, but his body betrayed him. The weight of the place was too heavy, too oppressive. He was trapped, and he knew it.

His hand reached out, trembling, to touch the stone wall beside him. The rough surface felt solid, cold—almost alive, like it was pulsing with energy, humming beneath his fingertips. He jerked his hand away, but the feeling lingered, vibrating in his bones.

Suddenly, a sharp, piercing noise cut through the stillness. The sound of metal scraping against stone. Jason's heart skipped a beat. His eyes darted to the far side of the room, where a shadowy figure stood in the doorway, just beyond the reach of the dim light. The figure was tall, its features obscured by darkness. But the presence of it was unmistakable. It was here.

A voice, soft and deadly, drifted toward him like a breeze through the cracks of a decaying house.

"Do you think you can run from the truth, Jason?" The words were like a knife, cutting through the tension, and Jason felt the air grow colder around him. "There's nowhere to hide now."

He gritted his teeth, refusing to let the fear consume him. His mind raced for a plan—any plan—but there was nothing. No options. Only the endless shadows that surrounded him, closing in with each breath he took.

The figure stepped forward, its form becoming more defined as it entered the light. Jason's eyes widened as he recognized the shape of the person in front of him. It was her.

Elle.

But no, it wasn't. Not truly.

This wasn't the woman he had once known. This was something else—something darker, something that wore her face but twisted it into a mask of cruelty and malice. Her eyes gleamed with an unnatural light, and the smile on her lips was twisted, as though it had been carved there by something far more sinister.

"You've always been so sure of yourself, Jason," she said, her voice dripping with mockery. "So certain that you could outsmart the darkness. But you've underestimated me. Underestimated us."

Jason's stomach churned. He backed up slowly, his body stiff with fear, but there was no place to go. The walls were too close, the room too small. He was trapped in a cage, and Elle—the thing that wore her face—was the key to it.

"You're not her," Jason whispered, his voice hoarse, barely a breath. "You're not her."

The creature that had once been Elle tilted its head, its lips stretching into a grin that was almost too wide, too unnatural to be human.

"No, Jason. I'm everything you've denied. Everything you've buried. The darkness inside you, inside us all. You've always been part of it. Always will be."

Jason's knees buckled, and he fell to the ground, his hands splayed out in front of him as if trying to catch his breath. He couldn't escape it. He couldn't escape the truth. Not anymore.

"You thought you could outrun this," the figure continued, its voice now louder, more forceful, filling the room with its presence. "But the truth always catches up. It always finds you."

Jason clenched his fists, the anger rising inside him. He wasn't going to give in. He couldn't. Not after everything he had been through.

"You can't control me," he spat, his words thick with defiance. "You can't control me, and you won't break me."

The creature's laugh was low, dangerous. "You've always thought that, haven't you? You've always thought you could fight it. But deep down, you know. You've known all along. You're just a part of the cage. And this cage, Jason, is made of your own mind."

Jason shook his head violently, trying to block out the words, but they burrowed deeper into his consciousness. He felt it then—something in the air, something in the room itself, tightening around him, like invisible chains wrapping around his chest, squeezing the air from his lungs. He gasped for breath, his throat closing up as if the very shadows were strangling him.

"You think this is real?" the creature sneered. "It's just a game. A trick. A reflection of what you've always been afraid of. You can't escape your own nature. It's too late for that."

Jason's vision blurred, and for a moment, he wondered if this was all just another nightmare. But it wasn't. The weight of it—

the suffocating air, the crushing darkness—was too real. Too tangible. His body was trembling, his hands slick with sweat, his mind spinning with every twisted word that fell from the creature's lips.

There was no escape.

And that thought, the realization of it, tore through him like a blade.

Jason had always believed that if he could just run—if he could just hide—he could outrun the darkness, outrun the truth. But the truth was that the darkness wasn't something out there. It wasn't some external force that could be vanquished. The darkness had always been inside him. He had always been its prisoner.

A wave of nausea washed over him as he fell to his knees, clutching at his chest. He was suffocating—not from lack of air, but from the suffocating realization that he had never really been free. That all along, he had been bound by the chains of his own mind.

The figure that wore Elle's face stepped closer, its dark eyes never leaving his. "You see now, don't you? You always have."

Jason opened his mouth to speak, but no words came out. Instead, a deep, guttural sound—something primal—rumbled from his throat. A sound of desperation, of defeat.

The creature smiled.

"You are mine now," it said, its voice a whisper of poison. "And you always were."

Jason's vision dimmed, and he felt his body giving way, as if all the strength, all the fight, was draining from him. The weight of the truth—of the cage he had built for himself—was too much to bear. And just as the shadows seemed to consume him, he closed his eyes, surrendering to the truth.

He had always been trapped.

He had never truly been free.

And now, it was too late to escape.

The walls closed in. And Jason was left alone in the darkness, locked within his own mind.

# 21

# The Mirror Shattered

*Jason's eyes flickered open, but the world around him remained a blur of fractured light. His head throbbed, as if it had been cracked open and left to bleed into the void. He was lying on the cold, rough surface of the floor again, his body aching with the remnants of his last desperate struggle. The stone beneath him was unyielding, pressing into his ribs like the weight of a thousand regrets. His breath was shallow, his throat tight from the darkness that had filled it just moments ago.*

But there was something different now. A shift in the air. A change. The oppressive weight of the room, the suffocating darkness that had nearly crushed him—*it was gone.* For the first time in what felt like forever, he could breathe freely, like the fog of despair that had gripped his chest had finally begun to lift.

He sat up slowly, his body stiff from the shock of the recent assault. His hands pressed against the stone, grounding himself as he tried to make sense of what had just happened. Had it been real? Was it a hallucination? The creature—the thing that wore Elle's face—it had seemed so real, so *alive*. But now... now, there was nothing. Only silence.

Jason's heart thudded in his chest as he looked around. The room was different from the one he had last seen. The walls were cracked, the stone crumbling in places as if time had forgotten this place. The air was no longer suffocating, but there was a sharp, electric edge to it, as though it was alive, watching him, waiting for him to make the next move.

His gaze drifted to the far corner, where a large, ornate mirror stood—tall, its frame intricately carved with symbols that looked both ancient and *wrong*. The mirror seemed to hum with an energy he couldn't place, its surface reflecting not the dim, crumbling room around him, but a perfectly polished image. An image of himself.

Jason's breath caught in his throat. He had seen that face before, of course. It was his own reflection, but somehow it felt *off*. The way the light hit it, the expression frozen on his face—it was as though the mirror wasn't showing him at all. It was showing something darker. Something deeper.

He stood on shaky legs, the instinct to move closer to the mirror rising within him. Every step felt like it was carrying him deeper into a trap, yet he couldn't stop. His feet carried him forward as if they had a mind of their own, the pull of the mirror irresistible. As he approached, he saw the edges of the reflection flicker, distorting like ripples on water. His own face seemed to twist, the features shifting as though it was not him at all but someone else—someone *dangerous*.

Jason reached out a hand, almost against his will, to touch the glass. The moment his fingers brushed the surface, the reflection shifted violently. His own image was replaced by something else—a shadowed version of himself, a distorted, monstrous version, its eyes black holes that seemed to pull him in.

The reflection grinned.

Jason recoiled, stumbling backward, his heart racing in his chest. The mirror seemed to pulse with the same energy that had nearly swallowed him before. But this time, it was different. This time, the pull wasn't just in the room—it was inside him, burrowing deep into his mind, into his soul. The reflection in the mirror wasn't just a trick of light. It was something more. Something that had been waiting for him all along.

He backed away, but the reflection didn't move. It remained, frozen in place, its grin growing wider. The longer he stared at it, the more Jason felt the pull—like an invisible chain that tightened around his chest, dragging him toward the glass. He fought against it, tried to turn away, but his feet refused to obey him. His body was no longer his own.

"*You can't escape it,*" the reflection whispered, its voice a low, rasping sound that made Jason's skin crawl. "*It's always been here, Jason. In you. With you. You've always known the truth, but now... now it's time for you to see it.*"

Jason's breath hitched. His mind was screaming at him to fight, to run, but every inch of his body was frozen in place, unwilling to move. The room around him seemed to grow colder, the shadows stretching and reaching toward him like hands that were determined to drag him into the darkness.

"*Look at yourself,*" the reflection purred, its grin stretching impossibly wide. "*See the truth, Jason. You are no different from me. You are me. And I am you.*"

Jason felt a sudden wave of nausea hit him. His knees buckled, and he dropped to the floor, his hands pressed to his head as if trying to push the voice out. He couldn't think, couldn't breathe. The reflection—*it wasn't just a reflection*. It was something else entirely, something that had been a part of him all along, lurking just beneath the surface.

"You don't belong here," Jason muttered, his voice barely a whisper. "I'm not you. I'm not..."

But even as the words left his lips, he knew. He *knew* it was a lie.

The truth was, this... this creature in the mirror—it wasn't some external force, some twisted version of himself. No. It was the *truth*. The part of him he had always denied, the part of him that had never been buried, but had always lived in the shadow of his mind. The darkness. The monster.

And now, it was staring him in the face.

The reflection's eyes bored into him, black holes that seemed to devour everything. *"You can't outrun yourself, Jason,"* it whispered, its voice soft but laced with malice. *"You can't escape your own nature. You can't run from the truth any longer. This is who you are."*

Jason's heart thundered in his chest as he struggled to breathe. The mirror—it wasn't just a mirror. It was the *truth* staring back at him, the reflection of everything he had hidden away, every fear, every flaw, every dark thought he had buried beneath the surface. The things he had tried so desperately to outrun. But there was nowhere left to run.

The walls seemed to close in on him again, the shadows creeping toward him, pressing against his skin like cold fingers. He could feel it now—the pull of the darkness, the weight of the truth pressing in on him, suffocating him. He wasn't just fighting the mirror. He was fighting himself.

And the reflection in the glass grinned, its teeth sharp and predatory.

*"You're mine,"* it said softly. *"You always have been."*

Jason's mind reeled. He couldn't breathe. He couldn't think. All he could do was stare into the eyes of the creature that wore his face and accept what had always been true.

There was no escaping this. Not anymore.

With a final, deafening crack, the mirror shattered. The glass exploded outward, shards flying in every direction, slicing through the air. Jason's body tensed, instinctively shielding his eyes, but the pieces didn't cut him. No, they *pierced* him, like a thousand needles searing into his skin, into his soul.

The shards melted into the darkness, the room dissolving

with them, leaving Jason alone in the emptiness.
   And that was when he realized the truth.
   He was still here.
   Still trapped.
   But not in the room. Not in the mirror.
   *He was trapped inside himself.*

# 22

# The Shifting Faces

*Jason's breath came in shallow gasps as he stumbled through the narrow alley, the city around him alive with muffled sounds of distant traffic, the occasional shout, the low hum of a nearby streetlight flickering in the darkness. His pulse thrummed in his ears, every beat like a countdown, and his skin prickled with the feeling that he was being watched. He had stopped looking over his shoulder; he couldn't afford to. It would slow him down.*

*It's not real*, he told himself over and over again. *None of it is real.* But the doubt clawed at his chest, a weight that refused to lift. The images from earlier—Elle's face, distorted, flickering, changing shape—were burned into his mind. He couldn't shake the feeling that she was here, somewhere, just beyond his sight, pulling him deeper into whatever nightmare he had stumbled into.

Jason's footsteps echoed too loudly, the sound unnerving in the silence of the alley. He glanced up and saw the faint outline of a door at the far end, a sliver of light leaking from beneath it. The door had to lead somewhere, anywhere. He had to get out of this maze.

He moved faster, the door drawing closer, but as he neared it, something changed. The flickering light grew dimmer, the shadows longer, darker. The space around him seemed to shift, the walls of the alley stretching and narrowing, bending in on themselves. Jason hesitated, his breath catching in his throat. Hadn't he been here before?

*No*, he forced himself to think, gripping the handle of the door. *It's just your mind playing tricks on you.*

But as his hand touched the cold metal, the world around him seemed to warp again. The alley disappeared, replaced by something else—a hallway, a room, something unfamiliar. His heart skipped a beat, and his throat went dry. He stepped back, the door still in his hand, but now it felt wrong. The edges were too sharp, the handle too smooth. There was something... *off* about it.

A movement at the corner of his eye—he turned quickly, but there was nothing. He could have sworn he had seen a figure, a shadow, just out of view. But now, nothing but darkness.

Then, the voice came.

"*Jason.*"

It was soft at first, a whisper barely audible against the rising panic in his chest. But there was no mistaking it. It was Elle's voice.

He spun around, his pulse racing, but once again, he found nothing. Just the oppressive silence, the shadows that seemed to press in from every side. A laugh, light and mocking, echoed through his mind, sending a wave of nausea through his stomach.

"*Elle?*" His voice cracked as he spoke her name, desperate, pleading. "*Where are you? What's happening?*"

A cold breeze swept through the hallway—no, it wasn't a hallway. It was a room now, dimly lit by a single, flickering bulb hanging from the ceiling. The walls were cracked, peeling, as if the place had been abandoned for years. He stepped further inside, the door slamming shut behind him, locking him in.

His breathing grew shallow again as he took in the room. The floor was covered in dust, scattered with remnants of things long forgotten—broken furniture, torn papers, half-open books. Everything was covered in the same dark smudge, as though the place had been untouched by light for far too long.

And then, there was her.

Elle stood at the far corner of the room, her figure barely visible in the dim light, her back to him. Her hair, once perfect, was wild, disheveled. She didn't move. Didn't speak. She just stood there, like a statue, her presence more suffocating than the silence itself.

"*Elle?*" Jason's voice trembled as he took a step forward, every instinct screaming at him to turn and run, but his feet were frozen, unwilling to obey.

She turned slowly, her face coming into view.

And Jason's stomach lurched.

It wasn't Elle. Not exactly.

The face that stared back at him was familiar, but it was wrong—distorted, as though someone had taken her features and twisted them. Her eyes were hollow, black holes where the light couldn't escape. Her lips curled into a smile, but it was jagged, too wide, unnatural.

"*You always knew,*" the thing in Elle's form whispered. Her voice wasn't soft anymore—it was guttural, sharp. "*You were never meant to save me. You were meant to find yourself.*"

Jason took a step back, his heart pounding so loudly in his chest that it felt as though it might explode. "*No...*" he whispered, his voice breaking. "*You're not real. You're just a... a reflection.*"

The thing that wore Elle's face tilted its head, almost thoughtfully, as if considering him. "*I am real,*" it said. "*And so are you.*"

Suddenly, the room around him shifted again. The walls closed in, the ceiling descending like a collapsing tunnel, and the floor seemed to tilt beneath his feet. Jason stumbled, his heart racing as he tried to steady himself, but the room continued to warp and twist around him. His vision blurred, the shapes around him becoming distorted, jagged edges cutting through the air like knives.

And then, as though it had all been a dream, it stopped.

The room was gone. The hallway was gone. The door was gone. Everything had vanished.

Jason stood in the middle of an empty void.

The silence was deafening.

And then, slowly, faces began to appear in the darkness. At first, just glimpses—flickers of figures that seemed to shift with every blink. But as he focused, they became clearer. People, all of them, each one with a face he recognized: friends, family, strangers he'd met along the way. All of them staring at him, their eyes hollow, their expressions unreadable.

But one face stood out above the others.

Elle.

Her face was back to normal—peaceful, beautiful, untouched by the distortion he had seen earlier. But something in her eyes was different. There was sadness there now, a depth of sorrow that Jason had never seen before. A look of finality.

*"Why did you leave me, Jason?"* Elle's voice was soft, a whisper against the growing dread in his chest. *"Why couldn't you stay?"*

Jason's heart squeezed painfully, and he stepped toward her, his hand reaching out, trembling. *"I never wanted to leave you,"* he whispered. *"I never wanted any of this. I was just trying to save you. To save us."*

She didn't move.

The silence stretched between them, thick and suffocating, and the world seemed to fade into nothingness. Jason's hand dropped to his side, his mind swirling with confusion and fear, as everything around him fell away.

And then, from the darkness, came a new voice.

*"It's too late."*

It was a voice he recognized, though he couldn't place it at first. But as the words settled in his mind, he realized it was his own.

And in that moment, he understood.

The faces around him weren't reflections of the people he had known. They were pieces of himself—fragments of his own fractured soul. The face in front of him was not Elle's, nor was it anyone else's. It was his.

And the truth hit him like a wave, overwhelming, crushing.

*He was the one who had been lost all along.*

## 23

## The Echo of Her Name

The sound of footsteps echoed through the abandoned hall, reverberating off the cracked walls like whispers of ghosts from another time. Jason's heart raced with each step, his breath shallow as he moved cautiously through the darkened corridor. The air was thick with dust, and the faint scent of decay hung in the atmosphere, making his skin crawl. The walls seemed to close in on him with every passing moment, the faint flicker of light from his lantern casting long, ominous shadows.

He couldn't escape the feeling that someone was watching him—no, something—but whenever he turned around, there was nothing but the empty hallway stretching behind him, just like the one ahead.

Get it together, he told himself, trying to steady his nerves. It's just your mind playing tricks on you. Focus.

But the closer he got to the end of the hall, the heavier the atmosphere became. A strange pull in his chest seemed to draw him forward, an invisible force that beckoned him to move faster, to keep going, even though every instinct screamed for him to turn back.

A soft whisper broke the silence, faint but distinct, curling through the air like a tendril of smoke.

"Jason."

The voice was so familiar, so heartbreakingly real, that it sent a chill racing down his spine. He froze, his heart pounding in his chest. It was her.

Elle.

His fingers tightened around the lantern, his mind racing. Was she really here? After everything, after the nightmare he had endured, could this be real? He tried to speak, but the words caught in his throat.

"Jason..." The whisper came again, closer this time, and he could feel it against the back of his neck, hot and breathless.

Without thinking, his legs moved, carrying him toward the source of the voice, drawn by some irresistible force. The hall stretched out before him, endless and winding, as if it was never-ending. He could almost feel her presence now, like a magnetic field, pulling him in.

He rounded a corner, and there, at the far end of the hallway, he saw her.

Elle. Or at least, the image of her. She stood there, her back to him, bathed in a pale, ethereal light. Her silhouette was framed by the faded, tattered remnants of old curtains, the shadows dancing around her like ghosts of memories long forgotten. Her long hair cascaded down her back, and her delicate fingers rested against the cracked surface of the wall, as though she was waiting.

No, Jason's mind screamed. This can't be real.

He took a step forward, but before he could move another inch, the temperature in the room dropped sharply. His breath came out in clouds of mist, the cold seeping into his bones as if the very air was alive, and it was suffocating him. His pulse quickened, panic rising as the weight of the situation sank in.

Elle turned then. Slowly. Her eyes, wide and empty, fixed on him with an intensity that made his blood run cold. There was nothing behind them. No warmth. No familiarity. Only a hollow, endless void.

"Jason..." The way she said his name was wrong. It wasn't her voice. It wasn't the voice he remembered. It was something darker, distorted, as if the very essence of her had been twisted into something unrecognizable.

Her lips parted in a grotesque smile, one that stretched far too wide, revealing teeth that were unnaturally sharp, jagged like broken glass.

"You've been looking for me, haven't you?" Her voice was a

mixture of sweet seduction and cold malice. "You think you can save me? You think you can fix what's broken?"

Jason's throat tightened, but he forced himself to speak. "What happened to you? What is this?"

Her smile deepened, her gaze turning colder, darker, and she took a step closer to him. The floorboards groaned beneath her weight, the sound chilling, as if the entire house was alive and moving with her. "I'm not the one who's broken, Jason. You've always known what I am, what I've always been. You just haven't wanted to see it."

Jason's chest tightened as the words sunk in. There was something about her—something wrong—and it was worse than the fear he had felt before. This wasn't the Elle he had loved. This wasn't even her in any sense he could understand.

She took another step toward him, and the air around him grew heavier, thicker, until he could barely breathe. The shadows in the room seemed to reach for him, stretching toward him like tendrils, curling around his body, tightening with every passing second.

"I don't understand," Jason gasped, stumbling backward, his mind struggling to comprehend what he was seeing. "You're not real. This can't be real."

Elle's head tilted to the side, and for a moment, her expression softened, though the emptiness in her eyes remained. "You've always been so good at pretending, Jason." She whispered the words as though they were a secret only they shared. "But you can't pretend anymore. The truth is here. It's always been here, inside you."

Jason's pulse was pounding in his ears now. Every instinct in his body screamed at him to get away, to run, but his legs refused to obey him. He was frozen in place, as if some invisible force had chained him to the ground.

Elle's form began to shift, her figure warping and distorting before his eyes. Her body blurred, the edges of her form rippling like water disturbed by a stone. The air around her crackled with a strange energy, and Jason could feel it—feel her—in his very bones.

"You think you can escape the darkness inside of you, Jason?" Her voice became deeper, more resonant, vibrating through his chest. "I am the echo of your own guilt. The shadows you've buried in the depths of your soul. You're mine. You always have been."

Jason's breath came in ragged gasps, and he felt his hands shaking. His entire body trembled with a fear so raw, so primal, that he couldn't control it. The shadows around him closed in tighter, the room now feeling like it was collapsing inward, and Elle's face—her face—began to twist into something horrifying, something monstrous.

"No," Jason whispered, the word barely escaping his lips. "This isn't real."

But even as he spoke, he knew it was. The terror. The darkness. The suffocating weight of it all.

Elle's twisted smile widened, and as she stepped forward again, her hand reaching toward him, the world around him seemed to break apart. The walls, the floor, the very air—it all shattered into fragments, like glass falling to the floor, splintering into pieces too small to see.

Jason screamed, but the sound was swallowed by the dark.

And then, there was nothing.

Just silence.

But in that silence, Jason could still hear her voice. A soft, faint whisper.

"You can't run from me."

# 24

## The Descent into Silence

Jason's pulse hammered in his ears as he stumbled forward through the blackened void, the weight of the air around him pressing down like a physical force. He couldn't breathe, couldn't think—only run. His feet pounded against the unseen ground, his body driven by nothing more than instinct. The world around him was an endless expanse of nothingness, a vast chasm where even sound itself seemed to be consumed by the oppressive dark. He was alone. Alone in this suffocating silence, save for the echo of his own breath and the clattering of his heartbeat, each pulse a reminder that he was still here. Still alive.

But for how much longer?

He had seen Elle—or had he? The memory of her twisted, broken form lingered in his mind, a haunting echo of something he couldn't grasp. Her words, her smile, the unnatural coldness in her voice—they all replayed over and over again, a relentless loop that twisted his thoughts into a knot of fear and confusion.

She had been there, hadn't she? She had called to him, led him here… but to what end?

The darkness around him seemed to deepen, the void swallowing the last remnants of the light from his lantern. Every step he took felt heavier than the last, as though the very ground beneath him was resisting, unwilling to let him move forward. His feet felt like lead, his legs aching, and yet he couldn't stop. He had to keep going. He had to escape. But escape from what? From Elle? From whatever he had become?

His mind reeled with the thoughts of the mirror, of the reflection of the monster that had worn his face. The thing that had spoken in Elle's voice, that had promised to consume him. He had tried to fight it, to outrun it, but every corner he turned, every time he thought he had outrun the shadows, they had followed. They had waited for him.

And now, in this vast, empty place, it felt as if the shadows were closing in on him again. He could feel their presence, feel them moving just outside his vision, waiting for him to falter, to slip.

Jason's breathing grew more erratic, the air growing thicker, colder, with each passing second. It was as though the silence itself was smothering him, cutting off his ability to think clearly.

No, he thought, forcing himself to stop. Don't lose yourself to the panic. Focus.

He tried to steady his breathing, his heart, but the more he tried, the more the silence seemed to press against him. It wasn't just the absence of sound. It was the feeling that the silence was watching, listening, waiting for him to crack.

The shadows at the edges of his vision flickered, just for a moment—too quick for him to be certain. But then there was another movement. No. Not a movement. A shape. Something in the distance, a figure just beyond his sight, standing at the edge of the blackness, its form indistinct, shifting in and out of view.

Jason's breath hitched, his instincts screaming at him to turn and run, to get as far away from whatever that was. But his body betrayed him, frozen in place. His gaze locked on the shape, the air growing colder with every second. It was a person—or at least it looked like a person. A figure in the dark.

Then, it spoke.

"Jason."

The voice was soft at first, a whisper that seemed to come from everywhere, from nowhere. It wasn't Elle's voice, not quite, but it carried a familiarity that sent a shiver down his spine. It was his own voice, but twisted, like the words were coming through a mouth he couldn't recognize, distorted by something dark.

"Jason…" the voice repeated, louder now, dragging the word out like a long, drawn-out breath. "Why are you still running?"

His blood ran cold.

He knew that voice.

It was him.

The figure in the distance began to take shape, slowly but surely, as though stepping out of the shadows, its form sharpening in the dim light. It was a version of him—a darker version. The figure's face was a cruel reflection of his own, distorted, twisted into something unrecognizable. Its eyes glowed with an unnatural light, black like the void, swirling with a depth that threatened to swallow him whole.

Jason's heart lurched as the figure took a step forward, its movement slow but deliberate. His body tensed, muscles locked in place as he instinctively took a step back, but the figure mirrored him, its movements a perfect reflection. Every time Jason moved, the figure followed, its presence growing closer with each passing second.

"You can't outrun yourself," the figure sneered, its voice echoing in Jason's mind. The words reverberated in the space between them, like a constant hum that made his head spin. "You've always known this, haven't you? You're not afraid of the dark, Jason. You're afraid of what you'll find when the light goes out. What you will become when the silence consumes you."

Jason's chest tightened as the words twisted in his mind, striking at the core of his deepest fears. It was right. Every time he had tried to run from the darkness, from the horrors lurking inside him, it had followed. He had been running from himself all along.

The figure's grin widened, a jagged smile that stretched too wide, its teeth sharp and unnatural. "You think you can escape, but you can't. The darkness is inside you, Jason. It's always been inside you. And now, it's all that's left. You've lost. You've always been lost."

Jason felt the ground beneath him tremble, a deep rumble that shook through his bones. The shadows seemed to grow, pressing in from all sides, consuming the space around him. He couldn't move. He couldn't breathe. The darkness was closing in, and no matter how hard he fought, he knew that it was too late.

The figure stepped closer, its face now inches from his own, its breath hot against his skin. "This is the end," it whispered, its voice a low rasp. "You're already in the dark, Jason. You always have been. There's no way out."

Jason's heart raced in his chest, the walls of reality bending around him as everything collapsed into the silence. The world around him shattered into nothingness, the darkness swallowing him whole, until there was no Jason, no figure, no sound.

Only the silence.

Only the cold.

And the echo of his own name.

# 25

# The Final Awakening

*The darkness receded, and for a brief moment, Jason thought he had escaped. The suffocating silence lifted, replaced by a flickering light in the distance. He could feel the weight of his own breath, the tremors still running through his body as his eyes adjusted to the dim glow that seemed to pulse and sway in time with his heartbeat. The air, once cold and oppressive, had warmed, and the overwhelming pressure that had threatened to crush him had lifted, though the fear still lingered in the corners of his mind.*

He took a step forward, the ground solid beneath his feet, and the light before him grew brighter, until it became a small, almost inviting glow at the end of a long corridor. It looked like the light from the doorway of a room—perhaps an exit. His feet moved of their own accord, one step after the other, driven by a flicker of hope that he hadn't felt in what seemed like forever.

As he drew closer to the light, his steps quickened, driven by an urgency that he couldn't quite explain. But the closer he got, the more the shadows behind him seemed to press in, silent, watching, as though they were waiting for him to make a mistake. His breath quickened, and though his legs urged him forward, a dark dread grew in the pit of his stomach. What if this was just another trap? What if the light was only another illusion, another cruel twist in a series of lies he had been chasing?

He reached the door, the light growing blinding in its intensity. His hand shook as he reached out to touch the handle. But before he could grasp it, a voice—soft, low, and familiar—whispered his name from behind him.

"Jason..."

His heart skipped a beat.

He froze.

It was her again.

Elle.

Her voice echoed in his mind, though he couldn't see her. He turned, slowly, but there was nothing in the darkness. Nothing at all. Yet the air felt thicker, heavier, as if she were there, watching, waiting. The silence pressed in, louder than ever.

"*Elle?*" His voice came out hoarse, cracking with the weight of all he had endured. "*Where are you?*"

There was no response, only the faintest sound—almost imperceptible—a soft rustling like the flutter of a page turning. It came from the shadows, the very ones that had been stalking him since he first felt their presence. His pulse quickened as he stepped away from the door, a sense of cold creeping down his spine.

Then, slowly, a figure emerged from the shadows. It was her. Elle.

But something was wrong.

Her eyes, once bright and full of life, were hollow now, black pools that swallowed the light. Her body was limp, as if she were a marionette with broken strings, moving with an unnatural, jerky motion. Her lips twisted into a thin smile, too wide, too unnatural, and her once-beautiful face now seemed distorted, warped by some unseen force. She was still Elle, but not Elle. The woman he had loved was gone, replaced by something else—something darker, something twisted.

"*Jason...*" Her voice was no longer soft and comforting. It was sharp, like a knife scraping across stone, and it cut through the silence like a scream trapped in his mind. "*Why did you leave me?*"

His heart clenched in his chest. He could feel the weight of her words like a suffocating force, crushing the air out of his lungs. "*I didn't leave you,*" he managed to say, his voice trembling. "*I've been searching for you. I'm trying to save you.*"

She shook her head slowly, the motion almost too fluid, too inhuman. "*There's nothing to save, Jason.*" Her voice dropped to a whisper, the words crawling through his mind, clawing at his sanity. "*I was never real. None of it was real. You've been chasing shadows, running from what's inside you.*"

Jason's chest tightened, and he took a step back. "No..." he whispered, his voice barely audible. "*That's not true. You're real.*"

Her smile widened impossibly, her face warping in ways that defied logic. "*I've always been a reflection of you, Jason. The darkness inside you. The lies you've told yourself. The things you've buried so deep that you can't remember them anymore. I'm the truth you've been running from.*"

The words hit him like a slap, and his legs threatened to give out beneath him. He couldn't breathe. Couldn't think. Couldn't move. The walls around him seemed to close in, the darkness pushing forward like a wave, threatening to drown him in its depth.

But then something shifted. A flicker of light—*real* light—pierced the blackness. For the briefest of moments, he saw something in Elle's eyes. A flash of recognition, of the woman he had loved, the woman he had known. It was there, hidden beneath the darkness. She was still in there. Somewhere.

"No!" he cried, his voice cracking as he stepped forward, reaching for her. "*Please... I can't lose you. Not like this.*"

But she recoiled, her face contorting with anger. "*You've already lost me,*" she hissed, her voice now a distorted snarl.

*"You've always been lost, Jason. This is who you are. This is what you've become."*

The ground beneath his feet trembled again, and the air thickened, pressing in on him from all sides. The door behind him—the light—flickered one last time, as if it were a beacon, calling to him. The escape he had been searching for was so close, so within reach. But the shadows were closing in again, faster this time, wrapping around his legs, pulling him backward.

The silence became deafening.

Jason's body moved before his mind could catch up. He stumbled backward toward the door, his breath ragged, his mind a whirl of panic. *"I can't stay here. I can't die here."* His hands gripped the handle of the door, his fingers slick with sweat, trembling as he turned it. But as the door swung open, it revealed nothing. Just more darkness, more silence.

He stepped through it anyway.

And fell.

The fall was endless, like gravity itself had betrayed him, dragging him deeper into the void, deeper into the unknown. His body twisted and turned in the darkness, every direction the same, every moment stretching into infinity.

But then, as the darkness consumed him completely, a voice—faint but clear—reached out through the abyss.

*"Jason..."*

It was her voice again. Elle.

And this time, it wasn't twisted. It wasn't distorted. It was real.

*"Jason... I'm still here..."*

And in that moment, as the darkness enveloped him, Jason realized one terrifying truth.

The journey had never been about finding Elle. It had always been about finding himself.

And now, finally, he understood.

www.ingramcontent.com/pod-product-compliance
Lightning Source LLC
LaVergne TN
LVHW011945070526
838202LV00054B/4811